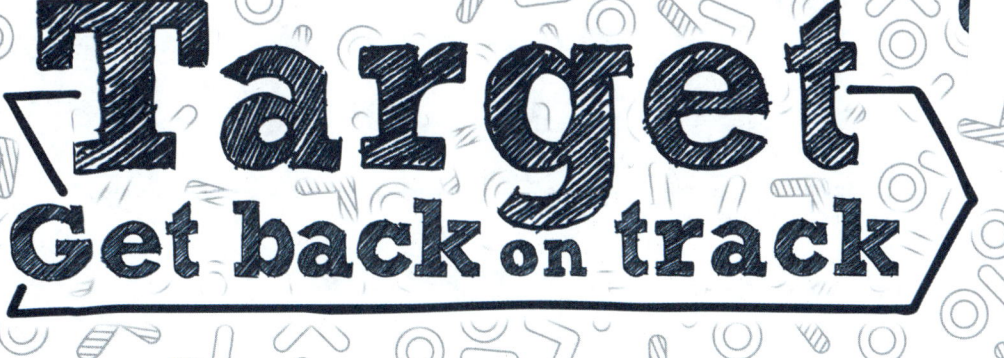

Target 5
Get back on track

AQA GCSE (9–1)
French
Reading

Danièle Bourdais
and Geneviève Talon

Pearson

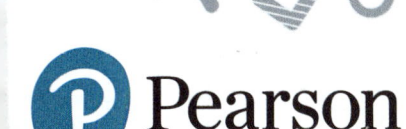

Published by Pearson Education Limited, 80 Strand, London, WC2R 0RL.

www.pearsonschoolsandfecolleges.co.uk

Text © Pearson Education Limited 2017
Produced by Out of House Publishing
Typeset by Newgen KnowledgeWorks Pvt. Ltd., Chennai, India

The rights of Danièle Bourdais and Geneviève Talon to be identified as authors of this work have been asserted by them in accordance with the Copyright, Designs and Patents Act 1988.

First published 2017

20 19 18
10 9 8 7 6 5 4 3 2

British Library Cataloguing in Publication Data
A catalogue record for this book is available from the British Library.

ISBN 978 0435 18909 9

Copyright notice
All rights reserved. No part of this publication may be reproduced in any form or by any means (including photocopying or storing it in any medium by electronic means and whether or not transiently or incidentally to some other use of this publication) without the written permission of the copyright owner, except in accordance with the provisions of the Copyright, Designs and Patents Act 1988 or under the terms of a licence issued by the Copyright Licensing Agency, Barnard's Inn, 86 Fetter Lane, London EC4A 1EN (www.cla.co.uk). Applications for the copyright owner's written permission should be addressed to the publisher.

Printed in Italy by L.E.G.O. S.p.A.

Note from the publisher
Pearson has robust editorial processes, including answer and fact checks, to ensure the accuracy of the content in this publication, and every effort is made to ensure this publication is free of errors. We are, however, only human, and occasionally errors do occur. Pearson is not liable for any misunderstandings that arise as a result of errors in this publication, but it is our priority to ensure that the content is accurate. If you spot an error, please do contact us at resourcescorrections@pearson.com so we can make sure it is corrected.

 This workbook has been developed using the Pearson Progression Map and Scale for French.

To find out more about the Progression Scale for French and to see how it relates to indicative GCSE 9–1 grades go to www.pearsonschools.co.uk/ProgressionServices

Helping you to formulate grade predictions, apply interventions and track progress.

Any reference to indicative grades in the Pearson Target Workbooks and Pearson Progression Services is not to be used as an accurate indicator of how a student will be awarded a grade for their GCSE exams.

You have told us that mapping the Steps from the Pearson Progression Maps to indicative grades will make it simpler for you to accumulate the evidence to formulate your own grade predictions, apply any interventions and track student progress. We're really excited about this work and its potential for helping teachers and students. It is, however, important to understand that this mapping is for guidance only, to support teachers' own predictions of progress and is not an accurate predictor of grades.

Our Pearson Progression Scale is criterion referenced. If a student can perform a task or demonstrate a skill, we say they are working at a certain Step according to the criteria. Teachers can mark assessments and issue results with reference to these criteria, which do not depend on the wider cohort in any given year. For GCSE exams, however, all Awarding Organisations set the grade boundaries with reference to the strength of the cohort in any given year. For more information about how this works please visit: https://www.gov.uk/government/news/setting-standards-for-new-gcses-in-2017

Contents

1 Recognising and understanding core vocabulary
Get started ... 2
1 How do I recognise and understand common words? ... 4
2 How do I show I have understood common words? ... 5
3 How do I take account of the context? ... 6
Your turn! ... 7
Review your skills ... 9

2 Recognising cognates and near-cognates
Get started ... 10
1 How do I recognise and understand cognates? ... 12
2 How do I recognise and understand near-cognates? ... 13
3 How do I identify false friends? ... 14
Your turn! ... 15
Review your skills ... 17

3 Synonyms and antonyms
Get started ... 18
1 How do I recognise synonyms? ... 20
2 How do I recognise antonyms? ... 21
3 How do I recognise words that belong to the same topic? ... 22
Your turn! ... 23
Review your skills ... 25

4 Identifying relevant information
Get started ... 26
1 How do I make sure I understand question words? ... 28
2 How do I locate answers in a text? ... 29
3 How do I avoid getting stuck on unfamiliar words? ... 30
Your turn! ... 31
Review your skills ... 33

5 Using grammatical clues
Get started ... 34
1 How do I understand the way words relate to each other in a sentence? ... 36
2 How do I make use of tenses to clarify meaning? ... 37
3 How do I make use of pronouns to clarify meaning? ... 38
Your turn! ... 39
Review your skills ... 41

6 Writing clear answers with appropriate detail
Get started ... 42
1 How do I avoid wrong, ambiguous and contradictory answers? ... 44
2 How do I make sure my answers are sufficiently detailed? ... 45
3 How do I avoid including irrelevant information? ... 46
Your turn! ... 47
Review your skills ... 49

7 Using deduction
Get started ... 50
1 How do I recognise positive and negative ideas? ... 52
2 How do I recognise opinions and justifications? ... 53
3 How do I answer questions by combining information from different parts of a text? ... 54
Your turn! ... 55
Review your skills ... 57

8 Translating accurately into English
Get started ... 58
1 How do I translate the meaning accurately? ... 60
2 How do I get the tenses right? ... 61
3 How do I write a clear and natural sounding translation? ... 62
Your turn! ... 63
Review your skills ... 65

9 Understanding unfamiliar language
Get started ... 66
1 How do I use clues from the whole context? ... 68
2 How do I use clues within the sentence? ... 69
3 How do I use clues from the unfamiliar words themselves? ... 70
Your turn! ... 71
Review your skills ... 73

Answers ... 74

Get started

1 Recognising and understanding core vocabulary

This unit will help you learn how to recognise and understand core vocabulary. The skills you will build are to:

- recognise and understand common words
- show that you have understood those words
- take account of the context.

In the exam, you will be asked to tackle reading tasks such as the ones on these two pages. This unit will prepare you to write your response to these questions.

Do not answer this question yet. You will be asked to come back to it at the end of the unit.

Exam-style question

Tweets about friendship

Your French exchange partner has posted a tweet about friendship on Twitter.

Read some of his followers' replies.

> **Lucas@Luka16**
> Il/Elle est comment, votre meilleur(e) ami(e)?

> **Maelys@Mael12**
> @Luka16
> Ce n'est pas facile d'accepter les imperfections des autres, mais ma meilleure copine est vraiment compréhensive. On discute de tout.

> **Mohamed@Mo_mo**
> @Luka16
> Mon ami et moi, on a les mêmes centres d'intérêt, comme la planche à voile. Malheureusement, il n'a pas le sens de l'humour, c'est dommage.

> **Adrien@AD99**
> @Luka16
> Mon meilleur copain est paresseux mais gentil. Il écoute mes problèmes et il respecte mes opinions. En plus, il est drôle et il me fait rire.

What do his followers say about their best friend?

For a **positive** view, write **P**. For a **negative** view, write **N**.

For a **positive and a negative** view, write **PN**.

1 Maelys   [N]   (1 mark)

2 Mohamed   [P]   (1 mark)

3 Adrien   [PN]   (1 mark)

Get started

1 In the exam-style question below, you will have to match the four notices with one of five English summaries (A–E). Choose **one** of these summaries and note down ✎ four or five relevant French words. Try to do this without reading the French text.

Example: **A** le match de foot, le joueur, …

....

....

Do not answer this question yet. You will be asked to come back to it at the end of the unit.

Exam-style question

Information notices

You see these notices about things to do in town on an information board in your exchange school in France.

What does each notice encourage you to do? Write the correct letter in each box.

A	Go to a football match
B	Go to the cinema
C	Go shopping
D	Go bowling
E	Go to a circus show

1 Ne ratez pas le spectacle Ragazzi. Les acrobates sont super! ☐ (1 mark)

2 Pour les amoureux du ballon rond: rendez-vous au stade samedi pour la rencontre Nantes–Toulouse. ☐ (1 mark)

3 On peut trouver des tee-shirts pas chers dans les boutiques du nouveau centre commercial. ☐ (1 mark)

4 Allez voir *Au revoir les enfants* au multiplexe. C'est une histoire triste avec de très bons acteurs. ☐ (1 mark)

The three key questions in the **skills boosts** will help you recognise and understand core vocabulary.

 How do I recognise and understand common words?

 How do I show I have understood common words?

 How do I take account of the context?

Unit 1 Recognising and understanding core vocabulary

Skills boost

1 How do I recognise and understand common words?

The starting point is to learn the meaning of words in topic-based vocabulary lists.

1 Some sources of vocabulary are more valuable than others. Draw lines to match the sources on the left with their value on the right.

One value on the right will be linked to two sources on the left.

- A in my French textbook, as a summary in each unit
- B in a glossary at the back of my French textbook, listed in alphabetical order
- C in lists handed out by my teacher as part of a lesson
- D in lists that I write out myself, for instance on cards or in a notebook
- E on a language learning app

- a good, as the action of noting down words can help you to remember them
- b OK, but not always relevant to the topics you have to study
- c good, as words are normally grouped by topic
- d OK, but words are not grouped by topic

2 Look at **1** again and tick ✓ your usual sources of vocabulary.

3 Look at this list of valuable techniques for learning vocabulary. Which ones do you normally use? Label them A for always, S for sometimes, N for never.

I use a bilingual list and …	A, S, or N?
I hide the English and try to remember what the French words mean.	
I hide the French and try to remember the words by looking at the English.	
I learn four or five words at a time.	
I learn phrases as well as single words.	
I also learn synonyms and antonyms.	
I write short French sentences containing the words I've learned.	
I work with a classmate and we test each other.	

4 These common words and phrases are to do with friendship, which is the topic of the exam-style question on page 1. Learn them using your favourite techniques from the list in **3**.

un(e) bon(ne) ami(e)	a good friend	il/elle …	he/she …
mon meilleur copain/	my best mate	écoute mes problèmes	listens to my problems
ma meilleure copine		discute de tout avec moi	talks about everything with me
compréhensif/-ive	understanding		
drôle	funny	accepte mes imperfections	accepts my faults
fidèle	loyal	respecte mes opinions	respects my opinions

4   Unit 1 Recognising and understanding core vocabulary

Skills boost

2 How do I show I have understood common words?

You don't have to understand every word when answering questions on a text. Focus on recognising and understanding the key words and the gist of the text.

1 Read the following texts quickly. What are the people's views on their friends? Write your initial impression in the box. For a positive view, write P. For a negative view, write N. For a positive and a negative view, write PN.

A Jules et moi, nous avons les mêmes centres d'intérêt, par exemple le sport. Il aime le tennis et je préfère la voile, <u>mais</u> nous adorons tous les deux le foot. <u>En plus,</u> il est fidèle et généreux.

B Yasmine est une fille très sympa parce qu'elle écoute mes secrets <u>mais</u> elle ne les répète pas! Elle est indépendante et <u>pas toujours</u> très patiente. <u>Par contre,</u> avec moi, elle est vraiment gentille.

C En classe, je travaille quelquefois avec Dylan, <u>mais</u> il est impatient si je ne comprends pas tout de suite et je trouve ça agaçant. Il est intelligent <u>mais aussi</u> arrogant.

D Samia est une copine très amusante. Le week-end, on va à la patinoire, c'est marrant. <u>Malheureusement,</u> elle est têtue et pas très sensible, mais je l'aime bien <u>quand même</u>.

2 Look for these common French phrases in texts A and B in **1**. Match them with the English.

nous avons les mêmes	we love
il aime	she listens to my secrets
je préfère	I prefer
nous adorons	she doesn't repeat them
elle écoute mes secrets	he likes
elle ne les répète pas	we've got the same

3 Some adverbs and connectives help you decide if the general impression is negative or positive. Find the underlined French equivalents of these phrases in the texts and write them down.

- **a** all the same   quand même
- **b** but (also) ....
- **c** by contrast ....
- **d** moreover ....
- **e** not always ....
- **f** unfortunately ....

4 In the space provided above the lines, label positive words or phrases in the texts P, negative ones N and a mix of both PN.

Unit 1 Recognising and understanding core vocabulary

Skills boost

3 How do I take account of the context?

Even with common words that you know, you have to pay attention to the context to get the meaning right. Be aware of homonyms – words that look the same but mean something different, such as *tour* in *Tour de France* and *tour Eiffel*.

1 a Read the text about two friends' day out and circle the correct meaning of the words in bold. Which word makes more sense in the context? The parts of the sentence most likely to help you are highlighted in the same colour as the word itself.

> Hier, j'ai passé une bonne journée avec ma copine Clara. Son grand frère est marié, sa **femme** [woman / wife] a un bateau et on est allés à la **pêche** [fishing / peach]. Clara a dit: «Éteins ton iPod! C'est trop **fort** [strong / loud], les poissons ont peur.» On a attrapé **neuf** [new / nine] sardines, c'est **beaucoup**! …

b Read the rest of the story and circle the correct meaning of the words in bold. Underline the parts of the sentence which help you make your choice.

> … Après, on a déjeuné à la pizzéria à côté de l'**hôtel de ville** [town hall / hotel]. Comme boisson, Clara a pris un **café** [café / coffee]. C'est trop **fort** [loud / strong] pour moi, je préfère le coca. On a regardé la **carte** [menu / map] et on a trouvé une «pizza pescatore», une pizza au poisson! Délicieux…
>
> C'était une journée amusante! Plus tard, je voudrais avoir mon **propre** [own / clean] bateau. D'abord, je dois gagner beaucoup d'argent parce que c'est **cher** [dear / expensive].

2 Look at the words in bold in each sentence. Write V for a verb in the present tense, PP for a past participle, N for a noun or A for an adjective. Then translate the sentences into English.

- **a** Il **porte** un pull.
- **b** C'est la **porte** d'entrée.
- **c** Elle dort dans un grand **lit**.
- **d** Elle **lit** un magazine.
- **e** Elle est **rentrée** à 19h.
- **f** La **rentrée** est le 3 septembre.
- **g** Il **court** vite.
- **h** Mon pantalon est **court**.
- **i** J'ai vu une **pièce** de théâtre.
- **j** J'ai une **pièce** d'un euro.

> When you try to understand a text, always look at the context, including the grammar. For example, a noun could have an article in front, a verb could have a personal pronoun.

Unit 1 Recognising and understanding core vocabulary

Your turn!

1 Circle Ⓐ the adjectives in the tweets. This will help you understand the overall meaning. An example has been done for you.

2 Highlight 🖊 adverbs and connectives in these tweets to help you sense the direction of the text. An example has been done for you.

> For each tweet, decide if it shows unconditional admiration, mixed admiration or no admiration at all. Look for clues.

Here is an exam-style question, which requires you to put into practice the skills you have worked on.

Exam-style question

Tweets about role models

Your French exchange partner has posted a tweet about role models on Twitter. Read some of her followers' replies.

Alicia@Astra16

Qui admirez-vous le plus, Malala Yousafzai, Adele ou Stella McCartney?

Léa@Loulou14

@Astra16

C'est Adele, une (excellente) chanteuse! **Mais** toujours des chansons tristes, c'est dommage. De plus, elle est riche mais quand même modeste.

Ali@Ali_Baba

@Astra16

Certainement pas Stella McCartney! Elle est célèbre parce que son père est hyper-célèbre, c'est clair. Elle n'a pas beaucoup de mérite.

Pauline@Pauline99

@Astra16

J'ai énormément d'admiration pour Malala. C'est juste une ado mais elle est très courageuse. En plus, elle est travailleuse et intelligente.

What do Alicia's followers say about the person they describe?

For a **positive** view, write P.

For a **negative** view, write N.

For a **positive and a negative** view, write PN.

1 Léa   ☐   (1 mark)

2 Ali   ☐   (1 mark)

3 Pauline   ☐   (1 mark)

> There are three tweets and three possible answers, but each answer can be used more than once or not at all.

Unit 1 Recognising and understanding core vocabulary

Your turn!

This is another exam-style question for you to try out the skills you have worked on in this unit.

Exam-style question

Messages from friends

While in France, you are making arrangements to go out with people you have met at your exchange school.

Which outing is each message about? Write the correct letter in each box.

A	Having lunch outdoors
B	Playing tennis
C	Going to the skatepark
D	Meeting up in town
E	Going to a friend's house

1. J'ai des balles mais emporte ta raquette. Il y a un court tout neuf à la salle omnisports! ☐ (1 mark)

2. Le Ritzy, c'est un café au centre, un endroit calme où se retrouver, et pas cher. ☐ (1 mark)

3. Tu veux venir chez Alexandre demain soir? Il est très fort avec les jeux vidéo! ☐ (1 mark)

4. Dimanche, on peut aller au lac de Mervent, si tu veux? On peut emporter un pique-nique et prendre le car. ☐ (1 mark)

Note that there are four short texts but five summaries (A–E). One of the summaries will not be needed.

Can you understand this phrase from the context? If not, can you still get the information you need from the rest of the sentence?

If you don't understand *un endroit calme*, can you get the gist from the rest of the sentence?

Get back on track

8 Unit 1 Recognising and understanding core vocabulary

Get back on track

Review your skills

Check up

Review your responses to the exam-style questions on pages 7 and 8. Tick ✓ the column to show how well you think you have done each of the following.

	Not quite ✓	Nearly there ✓	Got it! ✓
recognised and understood common words	☐	☐	☐
shown I have understood common words	☐	☐	☐
taken account of the context	☐	☐	☐

Need more practice?

Go back to pages 2 and 3 and answer ✎ the two exam-style questions there. Use the checklist below to help you.

Checklist Before I give my answers, have I …	✓
read the English introduction to the question to understand the context and predict the vocabulary?	
recognised common words (and if not, made a note to revise vocabulary by topic)?	
read through the text to understand the gist, making use of connectives and ignoring unnecessary words?	
used the context and the grammar to work out the meaning of homonyms?	

Always check if there are more possible answers than questions, as in the exam-style questions on pages 3 and 8. Bear in mind that one or more answers can be 'red herrings'.

How confident do you feel about each of these **skills**? Colour ✎ in the bars.

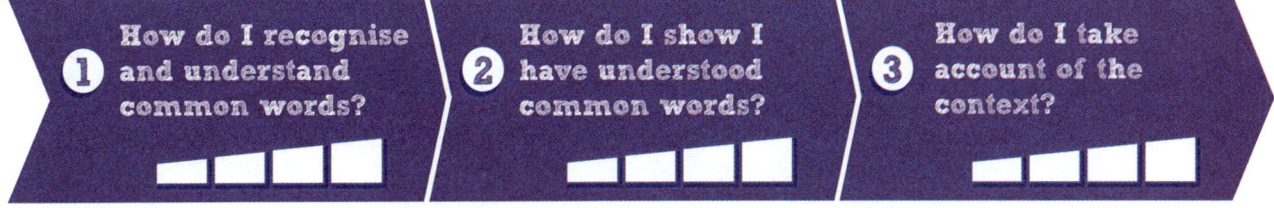

Unit 1 Recognising and understanding core vocabulary   9

Get started

② Recognising cognates and near-cognates

This unit will help you learn how to use cognates and near-cognates to make sense of texts. The skills you will build are to recognise and understand cognates and near-cognates, and to identify and be wary of false friends.

In the exam, you will be asked to tackle reading tasks such as the ones on these two pages. This unit will prepare you to understand different styles of texts, including extracts from literary texts.
Do not answer this question yet. You will be asked to come back to it at the end of the unit.

Exam-style question

Leisure time
Read the forum posts by francophone teenagers about their favourite pastimes.

> Je ne regarde pas souvent la télé, sauf les documentaires animaliers. Je ne rate jamais ces émissions-là. **Katia, 15 ans**

> Je n'ai pas beaucoup de temps libre le week-end parce que j'ai entraînement sportif. Je suis champion régional de course à pied! **Tristan, 14 ans**

> Moi, je suis bénévole dans un refuge pour chiens le week-end. Je m'occupe de chiens de toutes les races. **Malika, 16 ans**

> Je ne supporte pas le football à la télé. Moi, je préfère assister à tous les matchs de mon équipe au stade. **Clément, 15 ans**

> J'aime faire la fête avec les copains le week-end: on met de la musique, on danse, on s'amuse bien. **Josy, 17 ans**

> À la télé, je regarde tous les matchs de l'équipe de foot que je supporte. Par contre, j'évite les documentaires sur les animaux que je trouve ennuyeux. **Étienne, 14 ans**

Write the name of the correct person for each statement.

1 Who doesn't miss any TV programmes about animals?

(1 mark)

2 Who is busy racing at weekends?

(1 mark)

3 Who watches a lot of football on television?

(1 mark)

4 Who likes partying with friends?

(1 mark)

Get started

1. **a** Skim through the extract below and underline the words that you can understand because they are cognates or near-cognates.

   b Circle Ⓐ any false friends.

> Extracts from literary texts are like any other texts: use the same strategies for understanding and making sense of the meaning.

Do not answer this question yet. You will be asked to come back to it at the end of the unit.

Exam-style question

Read this extract from the novel *Un papillon dans la cité* by Gisèle Pineau.

> Féli is a young girl who leaves her life with her grandma on the French island of Guadeloupe to come and live with her mum in a Paris suburb. She becomes friends with Mo.

Mo m'a dit:
- Tu sais, Féli... j'ai une passion... comme Max. Lui, son rêve, c'est participer au tour cycliste de la Guadeloupe, devenir un grand champion. C'est pour ça qu'il passe son temps à attraper, nourrir et vendre des crabes pour s'acheter un vélo qui coûte au moins un million! Ma passion à moi... c'est la mer. Je crois que je vais essayer de devenir maître-nageur, Féli. J'voudrais apprendre à d'autres à aimer la mer. [...] T'as une passion, Féli?
[...]
- Bof! C'est pas vraiment une passion, tu sais. J'écris. J'écris tout ce qui m'arrive... J'ai un cahier pour ça.
- Tu parles de moi?
- Ouais!
- T'es super, Féli!

Which **two** statements are true? Write the correct letters in the boxes.

A	Mo dreams of becoming a racing cyclist.
B	Their friend Max sells crabs to earn money.
C	Mo talks about an inexpensive bike.
D	Mo loves the sea.
E	Féli writes about everything except her friends.

(2 marks)

The three key questions in the **skills boosts** will help you recognise cognates and near-cognates.

 1 How do I recognise and understand cognates?

 2 How do I recognise and understand near-cognates?

 3 How do I identify false friends?

Unit 2 Recognising cognates and near-cognates   11

Skills boost

1 How do I recognise and understand cognates?

When reading a text that appears difficult at first, always look out for words that are the same or similar (cognates) in both languages. This can help you make sense of the text.

> It is said that 45% of English words derive from French, which was used in Britain after the Norman Conquest of 1066. So English and French have a lot in common – good news!

1 Quickly read these texts about film and television. How easy to understand are they at first glance? Tick one of these boxes.

☐ very easy   ☐ fairly easy   ☐ quite difficult   ☐ very difficult

A C'est impossible de s'ennuyer pendant cette émission: le concept est très original, le reporter a du talent et avec lui, la culture devient passionnante!

B Nous avions une tradition familiale qui avait beaucoup d'importance quand j'étais petit: le samedi soir, on pouvait manger sur le sofa et regarder un feuilleton sur le petit écran! Quelle expérience!

C J'apprécie vraiment beaucoup les vieux films de science-fiction en noir et blanc: l'histoire était très simple mais ils avaient beaucoup d'impact sur le public dans les années cinquante.

2 a Read the three texts again. Underline Ⓐ all 15 words that look and mean the same in French and English.

b Translate ✏ texts A–C into English.

A ....
....
....

B ....
....
....

C ....
....
....

3 Words with the endings shown in the word box are often cognates. On paper, list ✏ as many French words as you can think of with each ending.

| -al   -ance   -ence   -ent   -ble   -ct   -tion |

> You need to be careful with this reading strategy as not all words that look the same or similar have the same meaning in both languages. Some are false friends, for example *émission* = (TV) programme, not emission.

12   Unit 2 Recognising cognates and near-cognates

Skills boost

2 How do I recognise and understand near-cognates?

There are thousands of words in French which, although they are not exactly the same as in English, are easy to understand if you are aware of some typical differences in spelling. These words are near-cognates.

1 a Read these sentences and highlight all the cognates or near-cognates you can find. Then write in the box how many you found in each sentence.

   i   Les spectateurs vont sûrement apprécier le monstre dans ce film. ☐

   ii Ce documentaire est relativement sérieux mais aussi très amusant et parfois comique. ☐

   iii Je suis très actif et je fais un sport individuel. ☐

   iv Les loisirs du futur? Le tourisme dans l'espace, une aventure inimaginable! ☐

   v   Ces vieux bâtiments historiques sont un peu étranges et pleins de mystère. ☐

   vi Pour être honnête, l'employeur ne va pas approuver ton sens de l'humour! ☐

   vii Le journaliste fait un commentaire sur la visite officielle du ministre. ☐

   viii Il préfère la réalité virtuelle d'un réseau social à la compagnie de ses amis. ☐

   ix Les problèmes techniques n'ont pas découragé les frères Lumière quand ils ont inventé le cinéma! ☐

b Translate the sentences on paper.

2 This table contains changes to word endings between French and English. Add further examples from the sentences above.

French	English	Examples from sentences
nouns		
consonant	add –e	futur/future,
-e	remove –e	visite/visit,
-e/-é, -i/-ie	-y	mystère/mystery,
-re	-er	monstre/monster,
nouns or adjectives		
-iste/-isme	-ist/-ism	tourisme/tourism,
-aire	-ary	documentaire/documentary,
-el(le)	-al	individuel/individual,
-que	-c/-ck/-k/-cal	comique/comical,
adverbs		
-(e)ment	-ly	sûrement/surely,

Unit 2 Recognising cognates and near-cognates   13

Skills boost

3 How do I identify false friends?

Cognates and near-cognates are 'good friends' which can help you, but you also need to be aware of false friends – words which look identical in both languages but mean something very different.

1 a Read this extract from a short story about two friends going on an outing. Then read the student's word-for-word translation below. You will soon notice that some of it doesn't make sense! Underline (A) the false friends in the French text.

b Correct the translation with words that make sense in the context.

> J'attends mon copain Hubert depuis un moment. Il est en retard pour notre journée au bord de la mer. Il arrive, il marche vers moi avec un pain sous le bras, et il crie joyeusement mon nom. Il a une veste marron trop grande pour lui. Il est petit, un peu gros, il a des boutons sur la figure mais il est très sympathique.
>
> Il n'y a pas de vélos de location alors nous achetons des billets pour le car et nous allons pique-niquer sur une plage très propre. Hubert m'offre une glace. Il demande quel parfum je voudrais. Il est si gentil! On reste un moment sur un banc, sous les pins, avec un joli chat noir.

I've been ~~attending~~ *waiting for* my friend Hubert for a moment. He is on retard for our journey at the seaside.

He arrives, he marches towards me with a pain under his bras and he joyfully cries my name.

He has a maroon vest too grand for him.

He is small, a bit gross, and has buttons all over his figure but he's very sympathetic.

There are no bikes on location so we buy tickets for the car and go for a picnic on a very proper beach.

Hubert offers me an ice-cream. He demands which perfume I'd like. He is so gentle.

We rest a moment on a bank, under some pins, with a jolly black chat.

2 Find the correct English translation for each of these common false friends in the word box and write it on the line.

| at the moment | bookshop | change/currency | high school | injured | meeting |
| occasion/opportunity/luck | second-hand | to sit an exam |

a actuellement ....
b blessé ....
c la chance ....
d le collège ....
e la librairie ....
f la monnaie ....
g d'occasion ....
h passer un examen ....
i la réunion ....

14 Unit 2 Recognising cognates and near-cognates

Your turn!

Get back on track

Here is an exam-style question, which requires you to put into practice the skills you have worked on, specifically how to use cognates and near-cognates to help you understand a text.

Exam-style question

All about books

Read this extract from the book *Haïti, Kenbe la !* by Rodney Saint-Éloi.

> […] Le douanier m'observe d'un air bizarre et m'apostrophe, en fixant la carte d'enregistrement et le passeport:
>
> - Destination Haïti.
>
> - Oui.
>
> - Pourquoi tous ces livres ?
>
> […]
>
> - C'est mon métier : écrire et fabriquer des livres.
>
> - Les autres ont du jambon, des spaghettis, des vêtements…
>
> - Ils mangent, ce qui est bien. Mais ils lisent aussi en Haïti.
>
> Le douanier, dans une pose d'étonnement, un doigt sur les lèvres, attrape un livre.
>
> […]
>
> Le douanier ouvre le livre avec curiosité et semble lire de brefs passages. Il sourit, détendu. J'ajoute :
>
> - Là-bas, il y a une grande soif de lecture, un grand besoin de livres. Je m'apprête à poursuivre pour affirmer que le livre est essentiel à l'hygiène de l'Haïtien. C'est l'île où le livre est sacré même pour les gens qui ne savent pas lire. […]

The author writes about his conversation with a customs officer at the airport during his trip back to the French-speaking island of Haïti after a devastating earthquake.

Make use of cognates or near-cognates to understand the text. Here, in the context of airport customs, *passeport* is likely to mean exactly the same as 'passport'.

Remember that the endings of words can give you a clue to their meaning. It's always worth applying the spelling rules you saw on page 13. Remember that the ending *-ité* is often *-ity* in English, so *curiosité* means 'curiosity'.

Beware of false friends! Does *lecture* mean the same in both languages?

Which **two** statements are true? Write the correct letters in the boxes.

A	The customs officer does not bother looking at the traveller's papers.
B	The traveller has a lot of food in his luggage.
C	The customs officer is curious about one of the traveller's books
D	The traveller is going to give lectures in Haiti.
E	The traveller thinks reading is vital for the people of Haiti.

(2 marks)

Unit 2 Recognising cognates and near-cognates

Your turn!

This is another exam-style question for you to try out the skills you have worked on in this unit – using cognates and near-cognates, and spotting false friends.

Exam-style question

Leisure and technology
A French website for teenagers has asked young people about their favourite pastimes. Read some of the responses it has received.

> Actuellement, je lis un roman sur ma tablette et c'est l'horreur! Je préfère lire un livre traditionnel.
> *Katya, 16 ans*

> Je n'ai pas vraiment de passe-temps. Je passe tout mon temps sur les réseaux sociaux: je suis accro.
> *Hugo, 16 ans*

> J'aimerais bien avoir une tablette, c'est très pratique quand on est malade au lit.
> *Morgane, 15 ans*

> Je télécharge des films sur mon portable mais je préfère aller au ciné. J'y vais avec mes amis.
> *Lucie, 16 ans*

> Je vais rarement au ciné car c'est toujours une déception: c'est cher et les gens font trop de bruit.
> *Chloé, 15 ans*

> Je ne supporte pas les réseaux sociaux parce que les nouvelles sont souvent fausses. Je préfère les actualités à la télé ou dans le journal.
> *Mathieu, 16 ans*

Write the name of the correct person for each statement.

1. Who would like to use electronic devices when they're unwell?

   (1 mark)

2. Who doesn't like using a tablet to read books?

   (1 mark)

3. Who doesn't like going to the cinema?

   (1 mark)

4. Who feels deceived by the news on social media?

   (1 mark)

Get back on track

Review your skills

Check up

Review your responses to the exam-style questions on pages 15 and 16. Tick ✓ the column to show how well you think you have done each of the following.

	Not quite	Nearly there	Got it!
recognised and understood cognates	☐	☐	☐
recognised and understood near-cognates	☐	☐	☐
identified false friends	☐	☐	☐

Need more practice?

Go back to pages 10 and 11 and answer ✎ the two exam-style questions there. Use the checklist below to help you.

Checklist Before I give my answers, have I …	✓
checked if there are any cognates that can help me understand the text?	
checked if there are words which I can easily understand if I adapt the spelling?	
checked if there are false friends I need to be careful of?	

> Remember to use your common sense when deciding whether a French word that looks like an English word means the same or not. You need to make sure it fits the context.

How confident do you feel about each of these **skills**? Colour ✎ in the bars.

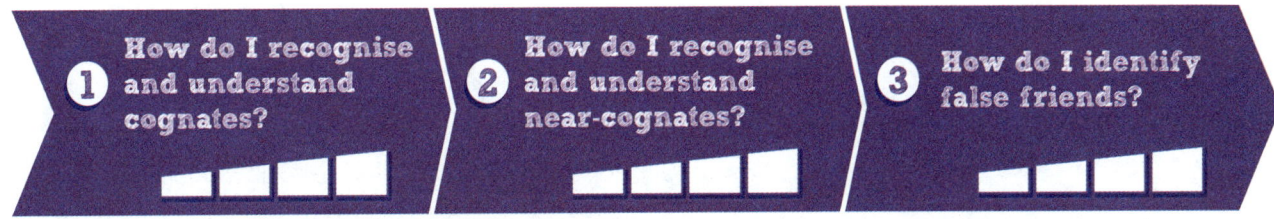

Unit 2 Recognising cognates and near-cognates   17

Get started

3 Synonyms and antonyms

This unit will help you learn how to make use of synonyms, antonyms and topic-based vocabulary. The skills you will build are to:

- recognise synonyms – words with similar meanings
- recognise antonyms – words with contrasting meanings
- recognise words that belong to the same topic.

In the exam, you will be asked to tackle reading tasks such as the ones on these two pages. This unit will prepare you to write your own response to these questions.
Do not answer this question yet. You will be asked to come back to it at the end of the unit.

Exam-style question

Daily life
Students from various French-speaking countries are applying for an exchange visit to your school and have sent messages describing aspects of their daily life.

Ma vie quotidienne
1. **Charles, Québec** Le matin, je prends le bus. Le trajet dure une heure, ce n'est pas relaxant! Si je me lève tard, je rate le bus et ma mère m'emmène en voiture.
2. **Sofia, Belgique** Pendant la semaine, je me lève tôt, je suis debout à 7 heures. Le week-end, je sors avec mes amis et je me couche tard. Le dimanche, par contre, je me lève vers 9 heures.
3. **Nathan, Nouvelle-Calédonie** Le soir après le collège, je fais mes devoirs. Je n'ai pas cours le samedi, mais je me lève de bonne heure car je dois réviser tout le week-end. C'est ennuyeux, je déteste ça!
4. **Énora, France** Le mercredi après-midi, je n'ai pas cours alors je me repose. J'aime le sport, alors le week-end, je joue au tennis, ça me déstresse.
5. **Aminata, Sénégal** Avant d'aller à l'école, je vais chercher de l'eau. C'est fatigant! Ensuite, je dois préparer le petit-déjeuner pour ma famille. Je travaille dur! À 7 heures 30, je pars au collège à pied.

Which message is about each of these aspects of daily life? Write the correct number in each box.

1 Helping at home   ☐ (1 mark)   3 Relaxing   ☐ (1 mark)

2 Using public transport ☐ (1 mark)   4 Studying   ☐ (1 mark)

> There are five messages but only four answers. Which message doesn't fit any of the answers?

Get started

1 Predicting topics is good preparation for understanding a text. You can see that this text is about celebrations. Note down ✎ the four or five most important celebrations in *your* life.

....

....

Do not answer this question yet. You will be asked to come back to it at the end of the unit.

Exam-style question

Celebrating

An online forum has posted a question on people's favourite occasions to celebrate.
Read some of the responses it has received.

Le sujet du jour: les fêtes
3 février, 14:40
Sondage spécial fêtes: Quelle est votre fête préférée?
Ma fête préférée, c'est mon anniversaire, parce que tous mes amis viennent. J'invite les copains du collège, les garçons du club de tennis et aussi mes cousins. **Amir**
Moi, j'aime beaucoup le 14 juillet parce qu'en général, il fait beau et on sort tard. J'adore danser dans la rue les soirs d'été! **Léa**
Moi, j'aime bien Noël. C'est super d'être dans une maison chaude et pleine de lumière quand il fait noir et froid dehors! **Justine**

Which of the following aspects is the most important for each person? Write the correct letter in each box.

A	Eating special food
B	Being cosy indoors
C	Being with friends
D	Receiving presents
E	Having fun outdoors
F	Wearing party clothes

1 Amir   ☐ (1 mark)

2 Léa   ☐ (1 mark)

3 Justine   ☐ (1 mark)

There are three messages but six possible answers. Three answers don't fit any of the messages.

The three key questions in the **skills boosts** will help you make use of synonyms and antonyms.

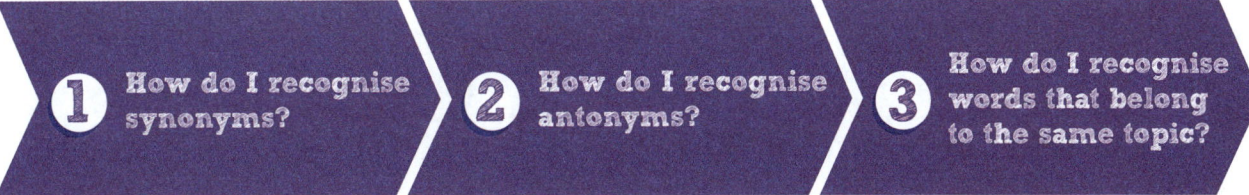

1 How do I recognise synonyms?

2 How do I recognise antonyms?

3 How do I recognise words that belong to the same topic?

Unit 3 Synonyms and antonyms   19

Skills boost

1 How do I recognise synonyms?

Synonyms are words with the same or similar meaning, for example *en ligne/sur Internet/sur un site web* or *gentil/sympa*. Reading comprehension exercises often rely on understanding synonyms, and recognising them helps you understand the gist of a text more quickly.
When you learn vocabulary, make a note of synonyms as you come across them.

1 Read these short messages. In each of them, find a pair of synonyms and note down ✏️ their meaning.

> All types of words can have synonyms. Here, look for nouns, adjectives or verbs.

a Beaucoup vont au collège en bus. Moi, je vais à l'école à pied parce que j'habite près.

au collège   à l'école   to school

b Le mercredi après-midi, je sors souvent avec mes copains. Par contre, j'ai des amis qui révisent.

copains

c J'adore le 14 juillet parce que j'aime beaucoup les feux d'artifice.

j'adore

d Pour la fête des Rois, on mange une galette. C'est un gâteau spécial et c'est délicieux.

e Le samedi, je regarde une série très intéressante à la télé. Les histoires de fantômes, c'est passionnant.

f J'ai horreur des barbecues parce qu'on sert de la viande, et je déteste ça.

2 Circle Ⓐ and replace ✏️ a word or phrase in the following sentences with a synonym from the box.

| à la salle de sport | à vélo | de fête | heureuse |
| mange | un ticket | tôt | une veste |

a Je me lève de bonne heure. ....
b Au petit déjeuner, je prends des céréales. ....
c Je vais au collège à bicyclette. ....
d En hiver, je porte un blouson. ....
e Le mercredi, je vais au gymnase. ....
f Le 14 juillet est un jour férié. ....
g J'ai un billet pour le concert. ....
h En septembre, ma sœur va se marier. Je suis contente! ....

Unit 3 Synonyms and antonyms

Skills boost

2 How do I recognise antonyms?

Antonyms are words with contrasting meanings, for example *facile/difficile*. Recognising antonyms helps you understand the gist of a text more quickly. When you come across antonyms, learn them.

1 What is the best way to shop: in town or online? Camille and Malika disagree! Read the dialogue.

  a i Highlight the first word in bold italics and write the English translation.

  ii Find the opposite word in the text; circle it and write the translation.

  b Repeat for all the words in italic.

> C: Moi, je trouve que le shopping en ligne, c'est **super**. Ça a beaucoup **d'avantages**.
>
> M: Je ne suis pas d'accord. Je trouve que c'est nul. Ça a beaucoup d'inconvénients.
>
> C: Mais faire les courses en ville, c'est **fatigant**! Faire son choix en ligne, c'est plus reposant.
>
> M: Parce que tu es **paresseuse**, peut-être! Moi, je suis active et **j'aime bien** sortir.
>
> C: Je déteste sortir dans les magasins, c'est vrai. Au centre commercial, c'est **cher**.
>
> M: Il y a des choses bon marché sur Internet, bien sûr, mais c'est souvent de **mauvaise** qualité.
>
> C: Il y a aussi des choses de bonne qualité sur le web! Et puis c'est pratique, les sites web sont toujours **ouverts**. Les magasins en ville, par contre, sont souvent fermés le dimanche.
>
> M: Les employés doivent **se reposer**, c'est normal. Ils ne peuvent pas travailler sans arrêt.

2 Ahmed goes shopping. Read his message, then sentences a–e underneath.

> *a* — Mes tennis sont très vieilles et aussi (trop petites). Je suis allé en ville pour acheter de nouvelles chaussures,
>
> *a* — d'une pointure (plus grande). J'habite loin du centre commercial, donc je suis allé dans une boutique en ville. Les magasins du centre commercial sont bon marché, c'est vrai, mais en ville, c'est plus près pour moi.
>
> Dans la boutique, j'ai essayé une paire de tennis pas chères mais vraiment démodées… Je n'étais pas content, alors le vendeur a apporté une autre paire, très à la mode.
>
> J'ai payé les chaussures 120 euros! C'est très cher et ça m'énerve, mais je suis heureux d'avoir une belle paire de tennis.

  i True or false? Tick the correct box and correct the false sentences on paper.

  ii For each sentence, circle the antonyms in the text that helped you decide whether it was true or false and label them with the relevant sentence number.

		True	False
a	Ahmed needed bigger shoes.	☐	☐
b	He lives close to the small shops in town.	☐	☐
c	The shops in town are not expensive.	☐	☐
d	Ahmed bought a fashionable pair of shoes.	☐	☐
e	He is happy with the price he paid.	☐	☐

Unit 3 Synonyms and antonyms   21

Skills boost

3 How do I recognise words that belong to the same topic?

When you learn vocabulary, practise using definitions in French. This will help you spot synonyms and near-synonyms and build up lists of words that belong to the same topic.

1 Draw lines to match the words on the left with their definitions on the right.

A les achats	a tout ce qu'on mange
B les boissons	b tout ce qu'on boit
C une casquette	c le repas de midi
D une ceinture	d un manteau pour la pluie
E le déjeuner	e un chapeau avec une visière
F un imperméable	f un accessoire pour tenir un pantalon ou une jupe
G la nourriture	g la taille ou la dimension des chaussures
H la pointure	h les courses, ce qu'on achète dans les magasins ou en ligne

2 Complete these definitions with a word from the box.

Think about the type of word that's needed: is it a noun, an adjective, a verb or an adverb?

| cher | d'habitude | détester | fête | fêter | magasin |
| marrant | ordre | plat | quelquefois | sucré | vert |

a le sapin – un arbre toujours ...., placé et décoré dans les maisons à Noël

b la dinde rôtie – un .... traditionnel à Noël

c la bougie – un objet qu'on allume avec une allumette pour une ....

d la charcuterie – un .... où on vend de la viande, surtout du porc

e la framboise – un petit fruit rouge, ... et parfumé

f .... – célébrer une occasion spéciale

g avoir horreur de – ...., ne pas aimer du tout

h ranger – mettre en ....

i .... – amusant

j bon marché – pas ....

k .... – normalement, en général

l parfois – ...., de temps en temps

22 Unit 3 Synonyms and antonyms

Your turn!

Get back on track

Here is an exam-style question, which requires you to put into practice the skills you have worked on.

1 As you prepare to answer this question, spot and circle (A):

   a three synonyms in posts 1 and 2

   b two synonyms in posts 3 and 5

   c two synonyms in post 5.

2 Answer ✏️ the exam-style question.

Exam-style question

Favourite celebrations

In an online forum, you read these posts about celebrations.

Qu'est-ce que c'est, votre fête préférée?
1. **L'Aïd** Pour l'Aïd, ma grand-mère va certainement préparer des pâtisseries au miel et à la fleur d'oranger. Tant mieux, parce que j'adore les gâteaux!
2. **Hanoukka** Chez moi, on va manger des beignets de pommes de terre et surtout, on va allumer beaucoup de bougies. C'est une fête très joyeuse!
3. **Pâques** Mes petits cousins viennent chez nous et je vais cacher des œufs dans le jardin. Ils vont bien s'amuser!
4. **La Saint-Sylvestre** Cette année, pour la première fois, je vais sortir avec mes amis. On va danser toute la soirée et à minuit, on va s'embrasser.
5. **Noël** Chez nous, à Noël, on offre quelque chose à tout le monde, aux amis, aux voisins, pas seulement aux membres de la famille. Je donne même un jouet à mon chien.

Which celebration would you join in if you enjoyed the following?

Write the number of the correct celebration in each box.

1 Playing with children   ☐ (1 mark)

2 Lots of light   ☐ (1 mark)

3 Eating sweet food   ☐ (1 mark)

4 Receiving presents   ☐ (1 mark)

Unit 3 Synonyms and antonyms

Your turn!

Get back on track

This is another exam-style question for you to try out the skills you have worked on in this unit.

1 As you prepare to answer this question, spot and circle Ⓐ:

- **a** a synonym for *me reposer*
- **b** a synonym for *fatigant*
- **c** an antonym for *tôt*
- **d** two antonyms for *travailler*
- **e** a definition of *j'aide ma mère*.

2 Answer ✏ the exam-style question.

Exam-style question

Weekend routine

The magazine 'À vous' has posted a question on its social network webpage.
Read some of the responses it has received.

À vous

3 mars, à 9h18

Sondage spécial Le week-end: Que faites-vous en général le week-end?

L'important pour moi, le week-end, c'est de me reposer et de me détendre. Je trouve les cours fatigants et le collège assez stressant!	Antoine
Le week-end, je me lève tôt et j'aide ma mère. Je range, je nettoie la salle de bains, je lave la voiture … Le soir, je suis fatiguée et je ne me couche pas tard.	Khadija
Le samedi, je fais mes devoirs et mes révisions. J'aimerais mieux me reposer, c'est vrai, mais j'ai des examens cette année, donc je dois travailler.	Clément

Which of the following phrases best describes each person's weekend? Write the correct letter in each box.

A	Helping at home
B	Relaxing
C	Going out with friends
D	Studying
E	Doing sport
F	Visiting family

1 Antoine ☐ (1 mark)

2 Khadija ☐ (1 mark)

3 Clément ☐ (1 mark)

> Remember that the texts may not use the exact French translations for the words in the summaries. Look for the English phrase that summarises the overall meaning of each text. Your knowledge of synonyms and words in the same topic will help with this.

24   Unit 3 Synonyms and antonyms

Review your skills

Check up

Review your response to the exam-style questions on pages 23 and 24. Tick ✓ the column to show how well you think you have done each of the following.

	Not quite ✓	Nearly there ✓	Got it! ✓
recognised synonyms	☐	☐	☐
recognised antonyms	☐	☐	☐
recognised words that belong to the same topic	☐	☐	☐

Need more practice?

Go back to pages 18 and 19 and do ✎ the two exam-style questions there. Use the checklist below to help you.

Checklist Before I give my answers, have I ...	✓
read the English introduction to the question in order to understand the context and predict the vocabulary?	
read through the text *and* the questions?	
looked for synonyms?	
looked for antonyms?	
identified sets of words that belong to the same topic?	

Always check if there are more texts than answers, as in the questions on pages 18 and 23, or more answers than texts, as in the questions on pages 19 and 24. This means some items are 'red herrings'.

How confident do you feel about each of these **skills**? Colour ✎ in the bars.

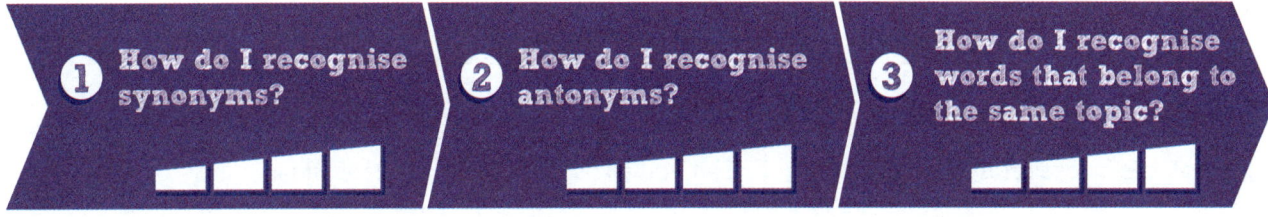

Unit 3 Synonyms and antonyms 25

Get started

④ Identifying relevant information

This unit will help you learn how to identify the information needed to answer the question. The skills you will build are to:

- make sure you understand question words
- locate answers in a text
- avoid getting stuck on unfamiliar words.

In the exam, you will be asked to do reading tasks similar to the ones on these two pages. This unit will prepare you to tackle these questions and choose or come up with the best answers.

Do not answer this question yet. You will be asked to come back to it at the end of the unit.

Exam-style question

Vannes, porte ouverte sur le golfe du Morbihan

Lisez ces informations sur les activités touristiques dans la ville de Vannes.

Château Gaillard: Musée d'Histoire de Vannes Collection d'objets préhistoriques Uniquement en juillet et août	**Golfe Croisières:** tour du golfe et visites des îles Du 1 avril au 30 septembre Prix réduits −15% pour familles nombreuses
Halles des Lices Produits locaux: fruits, légumes, produits de la mer Le mardi, mercredi, jeudi vendredi et dimanche De 8 h à 14 h Fermé le lundi	**Le Palais des Arts** Semaine du 7 au 13 juin à 19 heures: spectacle théâtral sur l'histoire de la Bretagne

Quel endroit recommandez-vous à ces personnes?

A	Château Gaillard
B	Golfe Croisières
C	Halles des Lices
D	Le Palais des Arts

Écrivez la bonne lettre dans chaque case. **Attention!** Vous pouvez utiliser la même lettre plus d'une fois.

1 Une personne qui veut acheter des produits de la région ☐ (1 mark)

2 Une personne qui aime sortir le soir ☐ (1 mark)

3 Une personne qui veut faire une promenade en mer ☐ (1 mark)

4 Une personne qui est à Vannes seulement en hiver ☐ (1 mark)

5 Une personne qui a beaucoup d'enfants ☐ (1 mark)

? Make sure you know exactly what the question is asking.

? Do you recognise the French question words? Can you spot one? What does it mean?

Get started

> You need to make sure you know where to locate the information needed and not panic if there are words you don't understand. Scan the text below briefly.

> You might not know the word *congénères*. Do you think you need to understand it to answer the questions? Would you be able to guess its meaning from the context?

Do not answer this question yet. You will be asked to come back to it at the end of the unit.

Exam-style question

You have come across this article about what young people think of urban or rural living.

> **Ville ou campagne?**
>
> Vous habitez en ville? À la campagne? Que préférez-vous?
>
> Nathan, comme la majorité de ses congénères au collège, adore la vie en ville, avec tous ses magasins et ses restaurants. Ce qui lui plaît le plus en ville, ce sont les installations sportives. Il sait qu'il y a des inconvénients comme les déchets dans la rue et dans les parcs mais ça ne le dérange pas vraiment.
>
> Céline, une camarade de classe de Nathan, aime bien les activités culturelles de la grande ville mais ne supporte pas le bruit. Selon elle, il n'y a rien de mieux qu'une promenade en forêt avec son chien.

1 What does Nathan like the most in his town?

A	the shops and restaurants
B	the sports facilities
C	the parks

Choose the correct answer to complete the sentence and write the letter in the box. (1 mark)

2 What doesn't Nathan really mind in his town? Answer in **English**.

....

(1 mark)

3 Céline prefers the countryside because …

A	she likes the cultural activities there
B	she can't stand the noise of the city
C	she has a dog

Choose the correct answer to complete the sentence and write the letter in the box. (1 mark)

The three key questions in the **skills boosts** will help you to identify relevant information to help you answer the question.

 1 How do I make sure I understand question words?

 2 How do I locate answers in a text?

 3 How do I avoid getting stuck on unfamiliar words?

Unit 4 Identifying relevant information 27

Skills boost

1 How do I make sure I understand question words?

If the question is written in English, make sure you find the exact information in the French text. If the question is in French, pay extra attention to the question words as some can be confusing.

1 Draw lines to match the English to the French question words.

A who	a où
B where	b qu'est-ce que
C when	c est-ce que
D how long	d pourquoi
E how	e quand
F why	f comment
G how much/many	g depuis quand
H what	h quel/quelle/quels/quelles + noun
I which	i combien (de)
J do/does...?	j qui

2 a Read each question below and circle the question word.
b Now match the questions to the answers by drawing lines to link them.

A Il y a combien de stades en ville?	a Ils préfèrent le rugby.
B Où est le stade en ville?	b Marc et Yann y vont.
C Qui va au stade ce soir?	c Oui, ils y vont ce soir.
D Qu'est-ce qu'ils vont faire au stade ce soir?	d Ils y vont en bus.
E Comment vont-ils au stade ce soir?	e Ils y vont depuis un an.
F Est-ce qu'ils vont au stade ce soir?	f Ils trouvent ça très amusant.
G Quand vont-ils au stade?	g Il y en a un.
H Depuis quand vont-il au stade?	h Ils y vont le samedi soir.
I Quel sport aiment-ils?	i Il est au centre-ville.
J Pourquoi aiment-ils ce sport?	j Ils vont jouer au rugby.

Unit 4 Identifying relevant information

Skills boost

2 How do I locate answers in a text?

In order to locate information in a text, remember that questions generally follow the order of the text. If you can't find the answer to one question but have located the answers to the questions before and after it, you are likely to locate the information needed somewhere in between.

Yannick parle de sa ville

- Où habites-tu, Yannick?

J'habite en Bretagne, à Hennebont, à une quinzaine de kilomètres de la mer. C'est une petite ville historique et touristique où on trouve le musée du Cheval, un endroit fantastique et unique si on aime les chevaux.

- Depuis quand habites-tu là?

Je suis né à Hennebont et les parents et grands-parents de mon père aussi! Ma mère par contre vient de Normandie, une région voisine.

- Qu'est-ce que tu aimes le plus là où tu habites?

Je crois que c'est la rivière qui passe au centre-ville, le Blavet, parce que j'adore faire du canoë-kayak. C'est mon sport préféré après la natation. Je vais aussi à la pêche en mer de temps en temps en été avec mon frère.

1 Read the text above. Decide which fact below comes first in the text and circle (A) **before** or **after** as appropriate. Then fill in each piece of information required.

> Look out for key words relating to the information you are looking for: here for instance, the name of the town (*Hennebont*), the word for 'sea' (*mer*) and the words to describe what kind of town it is (*petite ville historique et touristique*).

a How far Hennebont is from the sea   **before** / **after**   The kind of town it is

....

b How long Yannick has lived there   **before** / **after**   An attraction for animal lovers

....

c His favourite feature of Hennebont   **before** / **after**   His reason for liking the river

....

d His favourite sport   **before** / **after**   A pastime he does with his brother

....

2 Read through the question parts below then find the answers as quickly as you can from the text. Write the answers in French.

a the name of the region Yannick lives in   ....

b where his mother is from   ....

c if that region is far from Brittany   ....

d where the river is located in Hennebont   ....

e how often Yannick goes out to sea with his brother   ....

Unit 4 Identifying relevant information

Skills boost

3. How do I avoid getting stuck on unfamiliar words?

There are several strategies you can use to cope with words which you don't know at all in a text. One is to work out its meaning from the rest of the phrase or sentence it is in.

1) Read these six extracts from a weather forecast. Make sure you read the whole sentence. The words in bold might be unfamiliar to you. Circle (A) the words you know which can help you work out their meaning. Look at the example to help you.

A — Demain, le temps va **s'adoucir** et les (températures) vont (remonter), ce sera plus (agréable).

températures: how hot or cold it is *remonter*: *monter* means to go up *agréable*: pleasant

B — Attention aux **averses** en fin de matinée, n'oubliez pas votre parapluie!

C — Attendez-vous à des **gelées** matinales: tout va être blanc dans le jardin!

D — Après une matinée très nuageuse, nous allons voir le soleil avec de belles **éclaircies** l'après-midi.

E — Temps **couvert** toute la journée demain: on ne va pas du tout voir le soleil.

F — Après la **canicule** hier, gros orage ce matin: les températures vont être plus fraîches.

2) Circle (A) the correct translation.

a	s'adoucir	i to become warmer	ii to become colder	iii to become wetter
b	des averses	i strong winds	ii showers	iii snow falls
c	des gelées	i strong rain	ii storms	iii frost
d	des éclaircies	i clouds	ii sunny spells	iii fog patches
e	couvert	i overcast	ii cold	iii sunny
f	la canicule	i storm	ii cold spell	iii heatwave

3) a Read what these young people say about their town. There are words in bold you might not have come across. Circle (A) the words that help you work out their meaning, then annotate the words you've circled in English.

C'est une ville très [i] **accueillante**: les habitants sont très sympathiques avec les visiteurs.

Il y a beaucoup de [iii] **gratte-ciels** de plus de 56 étages. Du haut, la vue est super.

Il y a plein d'endroits [ii] **insolites** qui sont très intéressants parce qu'ils ne sont pas ordinaires.

Il y a des quartiers avec de jolis [iv] **pavillons**, ces petites maisons individuelles avec un petit jardin.

b Write the letter i–iv in the box next to each translation.

quirky ☐   detached houses ☐   skyscrapers ☐   welcoming ☐

30 Unit 4 Identifying relevant information

Your turn!

Get back on track

Here is an exam-style question which requires you to put into practice the skills you have worked on, specifically how to deal with unfamiliar words.

> Remember the practice you did on page 30 on using other words in the sentence to work out the meaning of unfamiliar words. Look at the words highlighted in the text: can they help you work out the meaning of *jour férié*? Which word(s) can help you understand 'baignades'?

Exam-style question

Enfants sportifs!

Lisez ces informations sur les activités sportives de la région.

A Centre équestre "Le Paldu" Quand? Ouvert d'avril à octobre (sauf jours fériés) Pour qui? Cours enfants (6–16 ans) Combien? Cours: 25 euros Séance d'initiation offerte aux enfants de 4 et 5 ans	**B** Piscine "La vague" Quand? Ouvert du lundi au dimanche (fermé les jours fériés) Combien? Cours de natation: 4–16 ans: 15 euros 16 ans+: 20 euros
C Parc d'accrobranche: "Les petits Écureuils" Quand? Ouvert uniquement les mercredis, week-ends, jours fériés et vacances scolaires Pour qui? Âge minimum: 4 ans; enfants accompagnés jusqu'à 16 ans Combien? Journée entière: 8 euros; demi-journée: 5 euros	**D** Club de plage Mickey Quand? Tous les jours en juillet-août, sauf le dimanche Pour qui? Enfants de 3 à 12 ans Quoi? Activités sportives, jeux d'équipe, beach ball, baignades en mer

Que recommendez-vous dans chaque cas? Vous pouvez utiliser la même lettre plus d'une fois.

1 Une activité pour une famille avec des enfants qui aiment les animaux ☐ (1 mark)

2 Une activité possible à faire toute l'année ☐ (1 mark)

3 Une activité gratuite ☐ (1 mark)

4 Une activité pour un enfant qui aime les activités de groupe ☐ (1 mark)

5 Une activité à faire un jour férié ☐ (1 mark)

Unit 4 Identifying relevant information

Get back on track

Your turn!

This is another exam-style question for you to try out the skills you have worked on in this unit.

> Think of the work you did on page 28 on French question words. Make sure you know the meaning of the highlighted French question words as they are key to the information given.

Exam-style question

You have come across Chloé's post online about how young people view tourism in their town.

> Êtes-vous d'accord pour encourager le tourisme dans votre ville?
>
> Un peu plus de la moitié des jeunes de ma ville sont favorables à l'augmentation du tourisme ici. Pourquoi? Ils estiment que cette activité est excellente pour l'économie et que grâce aux touristes, le centre-ville est plus vivant. Comment attirer les touristes? En créant un festival de musique dans le château. Quand les attirer? En basse saison, au début de l'hiver par exemple.
>
> Un petit nombre de jeunes n'ont pas vraiment d'opinion sur la question. Le reste trouve qu'au contraire, à cause des touristes, il y a plus de problèmes, comme la circulation. Selon eux, l'idéal est de faire des zones piétonnes au centre-ville et de construire un parking à l'extérieur de la ville. Je suis entièrement d'accord avec eux. Il faut aussi mettre des navettes électriques gratuites entre le parking et le centre-ville. Qu'en pensez-vous?

1 A little less than half the young people in Chloé's town

A	want to increase tourism in their town
B	want to decrease tourism in their town
C	have no opinion

Choose the correct answer to complete the sentence and write the letter in the box. (1 mark)

2 How do some young people suggest attracting more tourists? Answer in **English**.

....

(1 mark)

3 According to some young people, what is the main problem caused by tourism?

A	traffic congestion
B	having to build a car park
C	making the town centre a pedestrian zone

Choose the correct answer to complete the sentence and write the letter in the box. (1 mark)

4 What is Chloé's idea for improving tourists' access to her town? Answer in **English**.

....

(1 mark)

> On page 29, you practised scanning a text and locating the information you need. Remember that the questions usually follow the order of the text. Why not put a slash '/' at the end of the sentence where you found the answer to a question. It will save you time when you start looking for the answer to the next question!

32   Unit 4 Identifying relevant information

Review your skills

Check up

Review your response to the exam-style questions on pages 31 and 32. Tick ✓ the column to show how well you think you have done each of the following.

	Not quite ✓	Nearly there ✓	Got it! ✓
understood question words	☐	☐	☐
located answers in a text	☐	☐	☐
avoided getting stuck on unfamiliar words	☐	☐	☐

Need more practice?

Go back to pages 26 and 27 and do ✎ the two exam-style questions there. Use the checklist below to help you.

Checklist Before I give my answers, have I …	✓
understood the question words when relevant?	☐
scanned the text systematically in order to locate the information needed?	☐
made sure I know exactly what information I need to include?	☐

Never rush to tick or fill in an answer. Always check twice, even if the answer seems obvious at first: some options can be confusing and are meant to make you read the text very closely!

Get back on track

How confident do you feel about each of these **skills**? Colour ✎ in the bars.

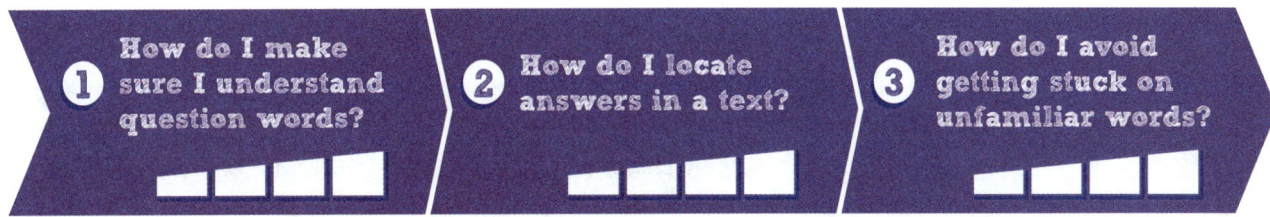

Unit 4 Identifying relevant information   33

Get started

⑤ Using grammatical clues

This unit will help you use grammar to understand a text. The skills you will build are to:

- understand the way words relate to each other in a sentence
- make use of tenses to clarify meaning
- make use of pronouns to clarify meaning.

In the exam, you will be asked to tackle reading tasks such as the ones on these two pages. This unit will prepare you to write your response to these questions.

Do not answer this question yet. You will be asked to come back to it at the end of the unit.

Exam-style question

Holidays

The Biarritz tourist office has published the results of a survey among its visitors. Read the summary of the results.

> Autrefois, Biarritz, au Pays basque, accueillait les rois et les empereurs. Maintenant, la ville ne reçoit pas que des célébrités. Voici les résultats de notre sondage auprès des touristes:
> - 3% des visiteurs ne vont pas passer les prochaines vacances à Biarritz car ils ne s'intéressent pas aux sports nautiques.
> - 8% pensent qu'il n'y a rien à faire le soir en ville.
> - 35% n'ont jamais fait de surf avant leur visite à Biarritz.
> - 40% n'y sont venus que pour le surf et les activités nautiques.
> - 58% déclarent qu'ils vont y revenir pour les prochaines vacances.
> - 62% allaient dans d'autres villes au bord de la mer, mais disent qu'ils se détendent mieux à Biarritz parce que c'est plus calme.

What percentage of visitors do the following?
Complete the boxes.

1 Say they will come back ☐ % **(1 mark)**

2 Enjoy the surfing ☐ % **(1 mark)**

3 Say there's no entertainment ☐ % **(1 mark)**

4 What is the most frequent comment? Answer in **English**.

....

(1 mark)

> The text contains six statements but there are only four questions. You will have to decide which two statements are irrelevant.

Get started

1 In a literary text, remember that dashes at the start of lines indicate a dialogue. Who are the two people talking? Write down ✏️ their names.

....

Do not answer this question yet. You will be asked to come back to it at the end of the unit.

Exam-style question

A holiday
Read this extract from *Le trésor de mon père* by Marie-Aude Murail and answer the questions which follow in **English**.

> Émilien is on a spring holiday at the seaside with his Uncle Marc.

> Marc voulait absolument que je l'admire sur sa planche, le lendemain.
> - [L'eau] doit être à −15°.
> - On va te louer une combinaison* au club.
> Donc, je me suis retrouvé à grelotter** […] pendant que mon oncle volait sur les vagues. Il faisait un temps sinistre, gris et venteux. […] J'ai pensé à l'été, aux cerfs-volants dans le soleil, aux vendeurs de beignets, […] aux détritus débordant des poubelles, […] et j'ai soudain trouvé très sympas cette plage vide, ce ciel noir, ce vent…

* combinaison – wet suit
** grelotter – to shiver

1 What does Marc want Émilien to do?

....

(1 mark)

2 Why isn't Émilien happy at the prospect of windsurfing?

....

(1 mark)

3 Where will Émilien get a wetsuit from?

....

(1 mark)

4 What does he think about the beach where his uncle is windsurfing?

....

(1 mark)

> An authentic text like this one can be harder to understand. Once you have enough clues to answer the four questions, you can ignore the rest of the text.
>
> If you are not sure you have understood enough to answer the questions, check you are clear about the pronouns (subject pronouns, reflexive pronouns, object pronouns) and about the tenses of the key verbs. For example, which object pronouns stand for Marc and for Émilien?

The three key questions in the **skills boosts** will help you to use grammar to understand a text.

1 How do I understand the way words relate to each other in a sentence?

2 How do I make use of tenses to clarify meaning?

3 How do I make use of pronouns to clarify meaning?

Unit 5 Using grammatical clues   35

Skills boost

1. How do I understand the way words relate to each other in a sentence?

Learn to recognise the building blocks of a sentence.

- Look for the verb and its subject; identify the complement or the descriptive word if there is one.
- Recognise more complex structures (*il dit que ...*, *elle pense que ...*).

> A complement is a word or phrase that completes a sentence:
> Lila va **à la plage**. Elle téléphone **à Yussef**, mais il visite **un musée**.

1 Mickaël talks about his sister Sophie and her holidays. Highlight the verbs, circle the subjects and underline the complements, as in the example.

Example: (Ma sœur Sophie) **a** un vélo.

a. Moi aussi, j'ai un vélo.
b. Je fais du vélo en vacances.
c. Cet été, je vais en Espagne.
d. J'emporte mon vélo et Sophie emporte sa planche à voile.
e. Sophie et moi, on adore le plein air!

2 Complete Mickaël's account of his holidays with the correct verb or subject from the box.

| dîne | fait | je | mon copain Jules | prend | retourne | retrouve |

Le soir, je rentre au camping, ... prends une douche, on .... vers 19 heures, puis je .... mes amis au café.

Quelquefois, on .... à la plage après le dîner et .... joue de la guitare. S'il .... chaud, on .... un bain de minuit.

> A sentence can have more than one verb:
> Pendant les vacances, je **me lève** à 8 heures et je **m'habille**.
> On **prend** le petit-déjeuner en famille, puis je **vais** à la plage.

3 The sentences below each consist of a main clause (in bold) and a subordinate clause. This pattern is often used to give an opinion. In each sentence, circle the word that always appears in this type of construction in French. Write down its English equivalent.

....

a. **Je pense que** la planche à voile, c'est très amusant. — I think that surfing is good fun.
b. **Elle dit qu'**elle veut retourner en Espagne. — She says she wants to go back to Spain.
c. **Il déclare qu'**il n'aime pas le vélo. — He declares he doesn't like cycling.
d. **Je trouve que** les vacances sont trop courtes. — I find that the holidays are too short.

36 **Unit 5 Using grammatical clues**

Skills boost

2. How do I make use of tenses to clarify meaning?

The texts you have to read often combine verbs that refer to the present, past and future. Make sure you are familiar with verb forms in all tenses, including the perfect and the imperfect.

1 Read Mickaël's account of a rainy day and complete it with past participles from the word box.

| bu | lu | mis | plu | pris | reçu | vu |

Hier, il a .... toute la journée. J'ai .... un message de Sophie. J'ai .... un chapeau, j'ai .... un parapluie et on a .... un chocolat chaud au café. Ensuite, on a .... le journal, puis on a .... un film au cinéma.

> A verb in the perfect tense is made up of two parts, usually a form of *avoir* + the **past participle**:
> - regular -er verb: *j'ai **emporté*** – I took
> - regular -ir verb: *tu as **fini*** – you finished
> - regular -re verb: *on a **répondu*** – we answered
> - irregular verb: *il a **fait*** – he did
>
> You also need to learn irregular past participles such as *boire*: **bu** by heart.

2 Circle (A) the verb *être* in the present tense and underline (A) the verbs in the perfect tense (*avoir* or *être* + past participle).

> Some verbs use a form of *être* instead of *avoir* to form the perfect tense: *je suis **allé**, elle s'est **habillée**...*

Example: Je (suis) fan de tennis, donc j'<u>ai acheté</u> un billet et je <u>suis allée</u> au championnat.

a) Younes est monté à la tour Eiffel et il a dit «Elle est très haute!»

b) Romain est gentil, il s'est levé à 7 heures et il a aidé sa mère.

c) Sara a fini la course cycliste à 14h30. Elle est rapide, elle est arrivée première.

3 Read the text, work out the imperfect endings and write them in the table.

> - Grand-mère, tu **faisais** du vélo quand tu **étais** petite?
> - Non, mes parents n'**étaient** pas riches, alors je **faisais** du patin à roulettes!
> - Vous **aviez** une voiture?
> - Non, nous **avions** une moto. Elle **était** belle mais pas très rapide.

je	tu	il/elle/on	nous	vous	ils/elles
-ais					

4 You can use *aller* + infinitive to talk about a future event. In these sentences, circle (A) the verb *aller* in the present tense and underline (A) the verbs in the near future, as in the example.

Example: L'été, en général, on (va) en Italie. Cette année, nous <u>allons visiter</u> Rome.

a) Le week-end, je vais à la piscine. Samedi, pour changer, je vais jouer au tennis.

b) Tu vas au bord de la mer avec Tom? Vous allez faire de la planche à voile?

c) Mes sœurs vont en ville parce qu'elles vont retrouver des copines.

d) Tu vas faire du camping cet été? – Oui, je vais acheter une tente aujourd'hui.

Skills boost

3 How do I make use of pronouns to clarify meaning?

Pronouns replace nouns. Learn to recognise the most frequently used pronouns.

1 a The text below uses common reflexive verbs. Circle Ⓐ the reflexive pronouns and underline Ⓐ the verbs.

b In the first column of boxes, note ✎ the tense (Pr = present, Perf = perfect, F = future). In the second column, note ✎ whether the phrase is positive (P), negative (N) or a question (Q).

Madame Dubois va (se) détendre au bord de la mer avec ses enfants, Jules et Aglaé:	F	P
«Aglaé, tu vas t'occuper du chien!»	☐	☐
«Les enfants, vous n'allez pas vous chamailler!»	☐	☐
Alors, est-ce que Madame Dubois s'est bien reposée à la plage?	☐	☐
Non, parce que Jules et Aglaé ne s'entendent pas du tout:	☐	☐
«Aglaé, tu ne t'es pas promenée avec le chien!»	☐	☐
«Et toi, Jules, tu ne te laves jamais!»	☐	☐
Ils se sont disputés toute la journée.	☐	☐

> You already know subject pronouns: *je, tu, il/elle/on, nous, vous, ils/elles*.
> In the following sentence, *je* stands for the speaker and *il* for *le train*:
> **Je** suis monté dans le train et **il** est parti tout de suite.
> Reflexive verbs use a second pronoun:
> *je* **me** *lève, tu* **te** *lèves, il/elle/on* **se** *lève, nous* **nous** *levons, vous* **vous** *levez, ils/elles* **se** *lèvent*.

2 Yaëlle explains what happened when she lost her purse in Paris. Circle Ⓐ the correct pronoun options. Use the table below to help you.

> Quand j'étais à Paris, j'ai perdu mon porte-monnaie. J'ai vu un agent de police et je **lui** / **l'** ai parlé. Il **l'** / **m'** a demandé: «Où **t'** / **l'** as-tu laissé?» J'ai dit que je **l'** / **lui** ai oublié dans le métro. Je **lui** / **m'** ai donné mon numéro de téléphone et l'agent **m'** / **l'** a dit: «Le bureau des objets trouvés va **l'** / **t'** appeler.» Je **l'** / **m'** ai remercié … mais le bureau ne **t'** / **m'** a jamais appelée. J'ai alors téléphoné à ma mère et je **la** / **lui** ai expliqué le problème. «Je vais **t'** / **l'** envoyer de l'argent», a-t-elle dit. Merci Maman!

> Don't confuse reflexive pronouns with object pronouns, which also appear in front of the verb.
>
> | direct object pronoun | indirect object pronoun |
> |---|---|
> | with verbs like *laisser, oublier, appeler, remercier*… | with verbs like *parler, demander, donner, dire, expliquer, envoyer*… |
> | *je* **te** *remercie* – I thank **you** | *je* **te** *parle* – I'm speaking **to you** |
> | *il* **me** *laisse* – he leaves **me** | *elle* **me** *demande* – she's asking **me** |
> | *je* **le/la** *remercie* – I thank **him/her** | *je* **lui** *dis* – I'm telling **him/her** |
>
> In front of a vowel, *me, te* and *le/la* become *m', t'* and *l'*: *elle* **m'***appelle, je* **t'***appelle, je* **l'***appelle*.

38   Unit 5 Using grammatical clues

Your turn!

Get back on track

Here is an exam-style question which requires you to put into practice the skills you have worked on, specifically how to use grammar to help you understand a text.

Exam-style question

Holiday accommodation

The manager of the *Plein Air* campsite has done a survey on holidaymakers' favourite accommodation. Read the summary of the results online.

> Voici ce que les visiteurs disent cette année sur leur hébergement de vacances:
>
> - 77% n'ont jamais dormi à l'hôtel parce qu'ils pensent que c'est trop cher.
> - 63% ne s'ennuient jamais en camping parce qu'il y a toujours quelque chose à faire.
> - 50% trouvent qu'il n'y avait pas beaucoup d'activités au camping *Plein Air*.
> - 45% vont revenir au camping l'année prochaine.
> - 30% vont aussi y revenir, mais ils ne veulent plus dormir sous la tente; ils préfèrent les caravanes.
> - 10% faisaient du camping quand ils étaient plus jeunes mais vont maintenant aller à l'hôtel.

Use the structure of the sentence as a clue. For example, in these two sentences find a main clause + subordinate clause used to express an opinion.

If you are not sure what some of these statements mean, ask yourself what tense(s) they are in: present, perfect, imperfect, future?

Pronouns sometimes hold the key to understanding. What does ils *stand for in this text?*

What percentage of people say the following?
Complete the boxes.

1. They are definitely coming back next year. ☐ % (1 mark)

2. They don't want to spend too much on holiday accommodation. ☐ % (1 mark)

3. They always find plenty to do at the campsite. ☐ % (1 mark)

4. What is the least frequent comment? Answer in **English**.

   ....

   (1 mark)

Unit 5 Using grammatical clues

Your turn!

This is another exam-style question for you to try out the skills you have worked on in this unit.

Exam-style question

A holiday

Back at school in October, Philippe tells his friend Jacques about his holidays.

Read this extract from *Silbermann* by Jacques de Lacretelle and answer the questions which follow in **English**.

> Hein! dit-il fièrement, je me suis bien bruni au soleil. C'est à Arcachon où j'ai passé le mois de septembre avec mon oncle Marc [...]. Toute la journée, pêche ou chasse en mer. Quelquefois nous partions à quatre heures du matin et nous rentrions à la nuit. [...] des courlis*... Il n'y a pas d'oiseaux [...] plus difficiles à tirer**. C'est mon oncle qui me l'a dit. Il n'en a tué que quatre pendant la saison [...].
> À Houlgate, pendant le mois d'août, [...] j'ai fait beaucoup de tennis. Mais, là-bas, c'était moins agréable [...]

Use your knowledge of pronouns – reflexive, direct object, indirect object – to understand the text. Remember, object pronouns go <u>before</u> the verb.

In a literary text, make the most of all the clues. Words starting with a capital letter, for example, are proper names, probably names of people or places.

There is a mix of verbs in the perfect and the imperfect in this text. Recognising this will help you make sense of the text.

* courlis – a type of seabird
** tirer – to shoot

1 How long did Philippe spend in Arcachon?

   ....

   (1 mark)

2 At what time did he sometimes leave in the morning?

   ....

   (1 mark)

3 How many birds did his uncle kill?

   ....

   (1 mark)

4 How did Philippe feel about his holiday in Houlgate?

   ....

   (1 mark)

Review your skills

Get back on track

Check up

Review your responses to the exam-style questions on pages 39 and 40. Tick ✓ the column to show how well you think you have done each of the following.

	Not quite ✓	Nearly there ✓	Got it! ✓
understood the way words relate to each other in a sentence	☐	☐	☐
made use of tenses to clarify meaning	☐	☐	☐
made use of pronouns to clarify meaning	☐	☐	☐

Need more practice?

Go back to pages 34 and 35 and do the two exam-style questions there. Use the checklist below to help you.

Checklist Before I give my answers, have I ...	✓
read the introduction to the question in order to understand the context and predict the vocabulary?	☐
read through the text *and* the questions?	☐
analysed the sentences, looking for verb, subject, complement or description, to help my understanding?	☐
identified the tenses in the sentences?	☐
identified pronouns (subject, reflexive, direct or indirect object) that can help make sense of the text?	☐

> In an exam situation, you're looking to answer the questions. Don't worry about the parts of the text that are not relevant to those questions.

How confident do you feel about each of these **skills**? Colour ✎ in the bars.

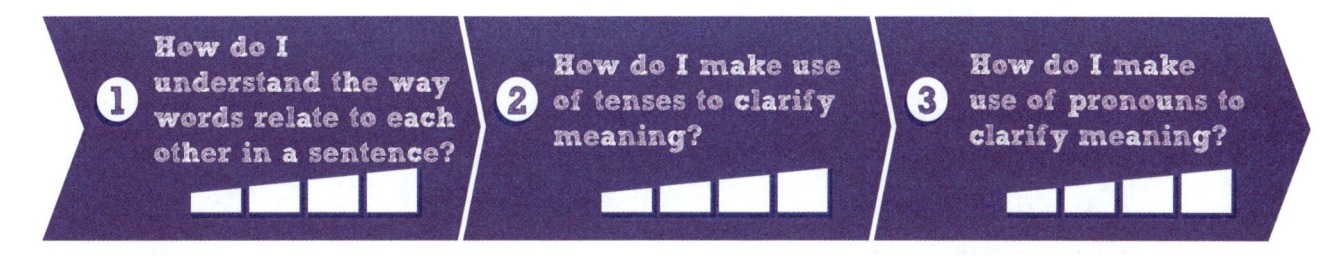

1. How do I understand the way words relate to each other in a sentence?
2. How do I make use of tenses to clarify meaning?
3. How do I make use of pronouns to clarify meaning?

Get started

6 Writing clear answers with appropriate detail

This unit will help you learn how to write your answers clearly and with just the amount of detail required. The skills you will build are to:

- avoid wrong, ambiguous and contradictory answers
- make sure your answers are sufficiently detailed
- avoid including irrelevant information.

In the exam, you will be asked to do reading tasks similar to these. This unit will prepare you to tackle these questions and write the best answers in English or in French.

1 You need to make sure that you understand the question words. Look at Question 2 below: what does the question word mean? Note down ✏️ as many other question words as you can remember from Unit 4.

....

....

Do not answer this question yet. You will be asked to come back to it at the end of the unit.

Exam-style question

Mon collège

Lucas vous envoie un e-mail. Lisez cet extrait.

> De : lucasd@email.com
>
> Sujet : Mon collège
>
> …
>
> Mon collège n'est pas mal, avec ses salles de classe modernes et bien équipées. Je trouve la cour de récréation vraiment trop petite pour y jouer au foot. Beaucoup n'aiment pas la cantine parce qu'ils disent que ce n'est pas bon. Moi, je la trouve bien car il y a du choix mais c'est un peu cher.
>
> Salut!
>
> Lucas

1 Quelle est la réponse correcte? Écrivez la bonne lettre dans la case.

A	Lucas trouve son collège moderne et bien équipé.
B	Il pense que la cour de récréation est parfaite.
C	Il joue au foot dans la cour à la récréation.

(1 mark)

2 Lucas aime la cantine. Pourquoi? Répondez en **français**.

....

(1 mark)

42   Unit 6 Writing clear answers with appropriate detail

Get started

> When answering the question type below, avoid writing too little as you risk not giving enough detail. You must also avoid writing too much as you risk being penalised for an ambiguous or unclear answer. Picking the exact information or detail required from the text is essential so make sure you understand what you are supposed to look for in the text.

(2) Look at the four questions in the exam-style question below. Note down what they mean in English.

....

....

....

Do not answer this question yet. You will be asked to come back to it at the end of the unit.

Exam-style question

Un e-mail

Lisez l'e-mail de Lucas qui parle de la forme. Répondez aux questions en **français**.

| De : lucasd@gmail.com |
| Sujet : La forme |
| … |
| Faire de l'exercice, ce n'est pas facile parce que je n'ai pas beaucoup de temps. Mes deux formes d'activité physique sont l'EPS au collège et l'entraînement de basket le samedi après-midi. Mais parfois je rate l'entraînement quand je dois aider ma mère à faire les courses. J'essaie aussi de faire attention à ce que je mange pour ne pas grossir. Je ne prends jamais de frites à la cantine et j'évite les desserts et les bonbons. J'ai décidé de devenir végétarien et j'ai aussi l'intention de m'inscrire à un club de gym quand j'aurai 18 ans. Et toi, comment restes-tu en forme? |

1 Pourquoi Lucas ne fait-il pas beaucoup de sport?

....

(1 mark)

2 Pourquoi ne va-t-il pas toujours à son entraînement de basket?

....

(1 mark)

3 Que fait-il pour ne pas prendre de poids? Donnez **deux** détails.

....

(2 marks)

4 Que voudrait-il faire à l'avenir pour rester en forme? Donnez **deux** détails.

....

(2 marks)

The three key questions in the **skills boosts** will help you to improve how you answer this type of question.

1 How do I avoid wrong, ambiguous and contradictory answers?

2 How do I make sure my answers are sufficiently detailed?

3 How do I avoid including irrelevant information?

Unit 6 Writing clear answers with appropriate detail   43

Skills boost

1 How do I avoid wrong, ambiguous and contradictory answers?

Your answers need to make sense. Make sure you know what the questions are asking, then select the appropriate information from the text. Read the whole text and use your common sense!

1 Look at the example text and question. A student has translated the questions and answers and annotated the answers to show why they are correct or not. Do ✏️ the same for texts a and b below on paper, choosing the correct option by ticking ✓ the box.

Example:

> Mon collège est super mais l'uniforme est obligatoire et il est horrible. Par contre, c'est pratique pour s'habiller le matin. **Pierre**

Just because a word appears in the text as well as in the question, it doesn't mean it's the answer.

Pourquoi Pierre met-il un uniforme? *Why does Pierre wear a uniform?*

- i ☐ parce que son collège est super — *because his school is great → doesn't make sense*
- ii ✓ parce que l'uniforme est obligatoire — *because the uniform is compulsory → correct answer*
- iii ☐ parce que l'uniforme est horrible — *because the uniform is horrible → doesn't make sense*
- iv ☐ parce que c'est pratique — *because it's practical → not the reason for having to wear it*

a

> Je n'ai pas pu faire le voyage scolaire en France avec ma classe cette année et j'étais vraiment très déçue parce que j'adore voyager avec ma classe, mais j'étais malade à ce moment-là. **Alina**

Pourquoi Alina n'a-t-elle pas fait le voyage scolaire avec sa classe?

- i ☐ parce qu'ils allaient en France
- ii ☐ parce qu'elle était très déçue
- iii ☐ parce qu'elle adore voyager avec sa classe
- iv ☐ parce qu'elle était malade

b

> Quand il fait beau, je vais au collège à pied parce que je veux bavarder avec mes copains et ça ne prend qu'une vingtaine de minutes, mais quand il pleut, ma mère m'emmène en voiture. **Théo**

Comment Théo va-t-il au collège quand il ne pleut pas?

- i ☐ à pied
- ii ☐ pour bavarder avec ses copains
- iii ☐ vingt minutes
- iv ☐ en voiture

44 Unit 6 Writing clear answers with appropriate detail

Skills boost

2 How do I make sure my answers are sufficiently detailed?

Your answers must give the exact information needed to answer the questions so you must ensure that you have included all relevant details from the text.

1 a Read what Zoé is proud of at school. Then read the questions and make sure you understand them by translating them on paper. An example has been done for you.

b Look at the corrector's comments, in red, for each answer and rewrite the answers, including all of the relevant information. An example has been done for you.

> Je suis fière de moi cette année. Tout d'abord, je suis contente car j'ai eu de bonnes notes dans les deux matières que je déteste le plus et que je trouve difficiles, les maths et les sciences.
>
> Mes parents étaient ravis de mes résultats et ils m'ont donné 50 euros d'argent de poche!
>
> De plus, j'ai participé à un échange scolaire en Espagne et c'était mon premier séjour à l'étranger sans mes parents. C'était génial: la famille chez qui j'étais était super sympa et j'ai fait de gros progrès en espagnol.
>
> En plus, j'étais membre du conseil d'administration et j'ai participé à l'organisation d'une rencontre sportive avec d'autres collèges pour récolter de l'argent pour une association humanitaire.
>
> Finalement, j'ai fait du sport: j'ai représenté mon collège au championnat régional de tennis et j'ai gagné tous mes matchs!

Example:
Pourquoi Zoé est-elle fière de ses bonnes notes en maths et en sciences? Donnez **deux** détails.

Why is Zoé proud of her good marks in maths and science?

Parce qu'elle est contente. wrong answer

Elle déteste ces matières et trouve ça difficile.

i Comment ses parents ont-il récompensé les notes de Zoé?

Ils étaient ravis. wrong answer

ii Qu'est-ce qu'elle a aimé pendant le voyage scolaire? Donnez **deux** détails.

La famille était sympa. incomplete answer

iii Quel était l'objectif de la rencontre sportive?

Rencontrer d'autres collèges wrong answer

iv Comment sait-on que Zoé est très sportive? Donnez **deux** détails.

Elle a représenté son collège au championnat régional de tennis. incomplete answer

> **Donnez deux détails** means 'give two details' so don't forget to do so!

Unit 6 Writing clear answers with appropriate detail 45

Skills boost

3 How do I avoid including irrelevant information?

When answering in French, make sure:
- you know where to look for the relevant information in the text to answer the question.
- you only lift the relevant information you need from the text. If you lift too many words, they might be irrelevant and your answer will become unclear.

1 Read this message from Martin about his school and questions A–E below. For each question, find the section of the text that contains the answer. Write the letter in the box after that section.

> Je trouve mon école très sympa. C'est un établissement privé pour garçons [A], dans la banlieue de Montréal [ ]. Notre journée commence à 8h30 et finit à 16h30. Nous avons des cours de 45 minutes [ ] et deux récréations d'un quart d'heure. Pendant la pause déjeuner qui dure une heure trente, je discute avec mes copains en mangeant à la cantine [ ] et on s'amuse à jouer un peu au foot dans la cour [ ]. L'après-midi, je suis fatigué mais après les cours, je vais aux répétitions de la chorale de l'école [ ] et je fais mes devoirs.

- **A** Dans quelle sorte d'école Martin va-t-il?
- **B** Où se trouve son école?
- **C** Combien de temps dure chaque leçon?
- **D** Que Martin fait-il avec ses copains pendant la pause déjeuner? Donnez **deux** détails.
- **E** Quelle activité extrascolaire Martin fait-il à l'école?

2 Read Chloé's message about her future school. Then look at the questions and the answers to them and strike out the information that is irrelevant. Explain why it is not relevant.

> Le trimestre prochain, je vais changer d'école. Je vais quitter mon collège et je vais aller dans un lycée international parce que je vais déménager aux États-Unis au mois de juillet. En effet, mon père a un nouveau travail à New York, une ville très intéressante. Apparemment, le règlement du lycée est très strict mais les profs sont sympa. J'espère que je vais me faire de nouveaux copains!

Example: Dans quel genre d'école Chloé va-t-elle étudier? – ~~Elle va quitter son collège et aller~~ dans un lycée international

the information about leaving her school is irrelevant as the question asks for the type of school

a Dans quel pays va-t-elle habiter? – aux États-Unis au mois de juillet

b Pourquoi va-t-elle habiter là-bas? – son père a un nouveau travail à New York, une ville très intéressante

c Comment est le règlement scolaire? – il est très strict mais les profs sont sympa

3 Now go back to **1** and answer the questions on paper.

46 Unit 6 Writing clear answers with appropriate detail

Your turn!

Get back on track

Here is an exam-style question which requires you to put into practice the skills you have worked on, specifically selecting or writing an answer in French by reading the text very closely and choosing the answer that makes the most sense.

Exam-style question

Au collège

Ariane poste un message sur un forum de jeunes. Lisez cet extrait.

> Sujet : Le redoublement
>
> …
>
> J'ai un an de retard au collège parce que j'ai redoublé ma sixième. Les profs ont dit à mes parents que je n'étais pas assez forte en maths. J'ai fait des progrès en maths pendant ma deuxième sixième mais j'ai beaucoup pleuré au début parce que je n'étais plus avec mes amies.

1 Quelle est la réponse correcte? Écrivez la bonne lettre dans la case.

A	Ariane arrive toujours en retard au collège.
B	Ses profs pensent qu'elle est assez bonne en maths.
C	Ses parents veulent qu'elle redouble la sixième.
D	Ariane s'est améliorée en maths après son redoublement.

(1 mark)

2 Ariane était très triste quand elle a redoublé. Pourquoi? Répondez en **français**.

....

....

....

(1 mark)

> Remember the work you did on page 44 to make sure you avoid picking or writing answers that are wrong, ambiguous or contradictory? Read the text very closely so you don't miss words that change the meaning of a sentence, such as negatives.

Unit 6 Writing clear answers with appropriate detail

Your turn!

Get back on track

This is another exam-style question for you to try out the skills you have worked on in this unit, specifically how to ensure that your answers are sufficiently detailed without including irrelevant information. Too little or too much information could cost you marks!

Exam-style question

Au collège

Lisez l'e-mail d'Antoine qui parle de son séjour chez son correspondant anglais. Répondez aux questions en **français**.

> De : antoine2@gmail.com
>
> Sujet : Un échange au collège
>
> Je suis allé trois jours dans le collège de mon correspondant Kevin à Londres, chez qui j'ai passé deux semaines. La journée à l'école était courte mais on devait prendre le bus tôt: le trajet était long vu que Kevin habitait assez loin.
>
> J'ai mis un uniforme et j'ai trouvé ça pratique parce que c'était facile de choisir les vêtements le matin et aussi très égalitaire, même si l'uniforme n'était pas très beau ni très confortable!
>
> Au collège de Kévin, j'ai trouvé super de manger un pique-nique dans une boîte au lieu d'aller à la cantine. J'ai aussi trouvé bien de quitter l'école à trois heures et demie. Par contre, ils ont cours le mercredi et les vacances d'été sont moins longues qu'ici.
>
> À bientôt!
>
> Antoine

1 Pendant combien de temps Antoine est-il resté en Angleterre?

....

(1 mark)

2 Le voyage en bus était-il court ou long? Pourquoi?

....

(1 mark)

3 Quels avantages Antoine a-t-il trouvés à l'uniforme scolaire? Donnez **deux** détails.

....

....

(2 marks)

4 Qu'est-ce qu'Antoine a particulièrement aimé au collège anglais? Donnez **deux** détails.

....

....

(2 marks)

> You can lift words from the French text but remember to change to *il* or *elle* if it says *je* in the text.

> Remember: if you are asked for two details, you must find two things to say!

48 Unit 6 Writing clear answers with appropriate detail

Get back on track

Review your skills

Check up

Review your responses to the exam-style questions on pages 47 and 48. Tick ✓ the column to show how well you think you have done each of the following.

	Not quite	Nearly there	Got it!
avoided wrong, ambiguous and contradictory answers	☐	☐	☐
made sure my answers are sufficiently detailed	☐	☐	☐
avoided including irrelevant information	☐	☐	☐

Need more practice?

Go back to pages 42 and 43 and answer ✏️ the two exam-style questions there. Use the checklist below to help you.

Checklist Before I give my answers, have I …	✓
understood the question fully?	☐
selected the relevant part of the text?	☐
avoided using words that are in the text but don't answer the question?	☐
given enough details to make sure the question is answered fully?	☐
been careful to avoid giving too much information that might be irrelevant?	☐
written *il* or *elle* instead of *je*?	☐

> When answering in French, you do not need to write in full sentences as it won't increase your mark. On the contrary, you might lose marks if you're not careful. Once you're confident you know the answer, write it in as few words as possible. You can re-use language from the text but do not copy a big chunk of it as it is unlikely to be fully relevant.

How confident do you feel about each of these **skills**? Colour in ✏️ the bars.

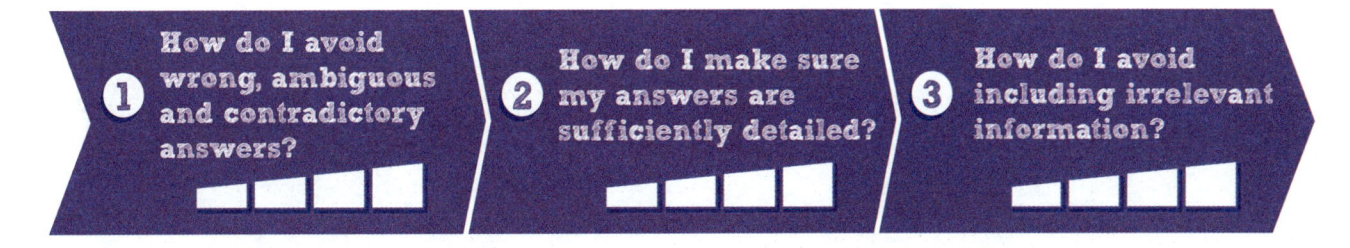

1. How do I avoid wrong, ambiguous and contradictory answers?
2. How do I make sure my answers are sufficiently detailed?
3. How do I avoid including irrelevant information?

Unit 6 Writing clear answers with appropriate detail

Get started

7 Using deduction

This unit will help you use your powers of deduction to understand information that is not completely explicit in a text. The skills you will build are to:

- recognise positive and negative ideas
- recognise opinions and justifications
- answer questions by combining information from different parts of a text.

In the exam, you will be asked to tackle reading tasks such as the ones on these two pages. This unit will prepare you to write your response to these questions.

Do not answer this question yet. You will be asked to come back to it at the end of the unit.

Exam-style question

Le travail

Lisez ces conseils dans le magazine *Votre avenir*.

> Travailler seul(e) ou avec d'autres? Quand on rentre dans la vie active, c'est une bonne idée de trouver un emploi dans une entreprise, même petite. On apprend ainsi beaucoup de choses et on profite de l'expérience de ses collègues. On reçoit aussi un salaire régulier, ce qui est un avantage. Si on est indépendant de caractère, plus tard on peut travailler seul(e). On peut alors développer sa créativité, sans patron.

> Si vous avez une passion, comme la musique ou le sport, vous avez peut-être envie de travailler dans ce secteur. C'est bien d'adorer son travail, mais il faut être réaliste et penser au salaire, aux risques de chômage… Parlez à des professionnels autour de vous.

1 Que conseille le magazine aux jeunes qui cherchent un premier travail?

Écrivez la bonne lettre dans la case.

A	Créer sa propre entreprise
B	Devenir employé(e)
C	Continuer à étudier

(1 mark)

2 Dans le deuxième paragraphe, qu'est-ce que le message recommande **exactement**?

Écrivez la bonne lettre dans la case.

A	Obtenir plus de renseignements
B	Choisir un travail qu'on aime
C	Trouver un travail bien payé

(1 mark)

Remember that reading the questions is just as important as reading the text. Focus on what the questions are asking you to find and ignore material in the text that is not relevant.

Get started

1 The introduction to the exam-style question below says *Mariana parle de ses projets sur son blog.* Which form do you expect the verbs to be in? Tick ✓ the appropriate box.

a mostly in the first person (*je* vais aller…) ☐

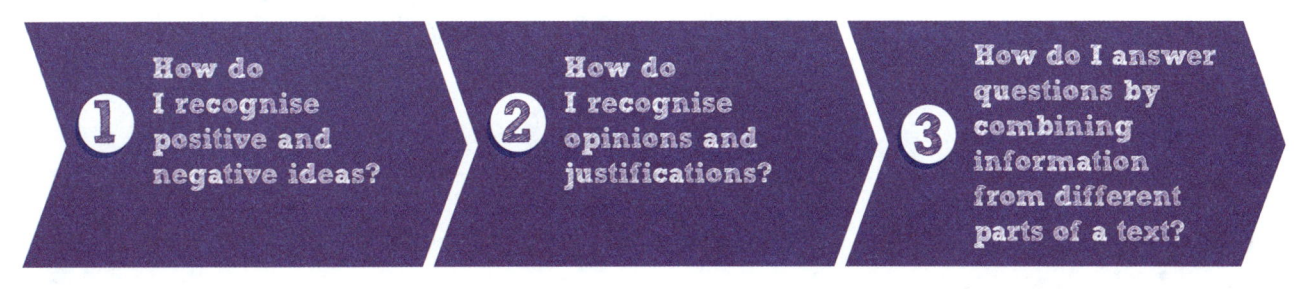

b mostly in the third person (*elle* va aller…) ☐

Do not answer this question yet. You will be asked to come back to it at the end of the unit.

Exam-style question

Année sabbatique

Mariana parle de ses projets sur son blog.

> Après le lycée, je prendrai une année sabbatique et j'irai travailler à l'étranger. Ce sera une super expérience, parce que je n'ai jamais quitté la France! À part les visites en Espagne, bien sûr, pour aller voir mes grands-parents. J'aime bien pratiquer mon espagnol avec eux.
>
> Je voudrais partir avec l'organisation Odyssée. C'est bien de partir avec cette organisation parce qu'ils s'occupent des questions pratiques comme les avions, les trains, le logement… Par contre, ils n'aident pas à trouver du travail. Les jeunes doivent se débrouiller. Ce n'est pas facile, dans un pays étranger.
>
> Pour le pays, je n'ai pas encore décidé. Personnellement, j'aimerais l'Argentine, puisque je parle un peu la langue. D'un autre côté, il y a pas mal de violence en Amérique du Sud et ça inquiète mes parents.

1 Choisissez dans la liste un aspect **positif** et un aspect **négatif** de *l'organisation Odyssée*.

A	le prix
B	la langue
C	l'emploi
D	le transport
E	les dates

Écrivez les bonnes lettres dans les cases.

Positif ☐ Négatif ☐ (2 marks)

2 Mentionnez l'aspect **positif** de l'Argentine. Répondez en **français**.

....

(1 mark)

> Pay particular attention to words in the questions that are bold.

The three key questions in the **skills boosts** will help you use your powers of deduction to understand information that is not completely explicit in a text.

1 How do I recognise positive and negative ideas?

2 How do I recognise opinions and justifications?

3 How do I answer questions by combining information from different parts of a text?

Unit 7 Using deduction 51

Skills boost

1 How do I recognise positive and negative ideas?

In the texts you read, positive and negative ideas are not always explicit. That means they are not always expressed in a direct way.

1 Read these teenagers' opinions about part-time jobs. Look for the adjectives that could give you a clue to the writer's opinion and circle Ⓐ them, as in the example.

Pour promener les chiens, il faut aimer les animaux. Ce n'est pas bien payé mais l'avantage, c'est que c'est un travail en plein air et donc c'est (bon) pour la santé. **Inès**	Si on aime les enfants, on peut faire du baby-sitting. Ce n'est pas difficile, mais personnellement, je trouve ça ennuyeux. En plus, on est obligé de se coucher tard et par conséquent on est fatigué le lendemain. **Daoud**
Pendant les vacances, j'ai vendu des glaces à la plage. C'était un peu fatigant, mais j'ai gagné beaucoup d'argent et en plus, j'ai mangé beaucoup de glaces. J'adore ça! **Julien**	Au garage près de chez moi, on peut laver les voitures le week-end. L'été, ça va, mais l'hiver, par contre, ce n'est pas agréable d'avoir toujours les mains dans l'eau froide. **Lola**

2 Decide whether the adjectives in **1** point to a positive or a negative opinion. Watch out for the negative *ne ... pas*, which may give the adjective the opposite meaning. Write ✏ P or N above each adjective you have circled.

3 a There are usually other clues to a writer's opinion. In the first three texts, find the French for the phrases below and write ✏ them on the line. Then note ✏ whether each phase is positive (P), negative (N) or neutral (PN) in the box.

   i   I love it .... ☐

   ii I find it .... ☐

   iii you are obliged to .... ☐

   iv I earned a lot of money .... ☐

   v   the advantage is that .... ☐

b In Lola's text, which of these two phrases is a clue to a positive opinion and which one to a negative opinion? Note ✏ P or N in the box.

   ça va ☐   avoir toujours les mains dans l'eau froide ☐

4 Find the French equivalents of the connectives below in the texts and write ✏ them down on paper. Label ✏ them R for those that help reinforce a point and DD for those that take responses in a different direction.

   a as a result ☐   **d** on the other hand ☐
   b moreover ☐   **e** therefore ☐
   c personally ☐   **f** but ☐

52   Unit 7 Using deduction

Skills boost

2 How do I recognise opinions and justifications?

The texts you read often combine opinions with justifications, which are reasons or examples.
- If you are not sure you have understood the writer's opinion, look for reasons or examples that give you clues.
- Learn vocabulary that clearly signals a writer's opinion, such as *heureusement/malheureusement*.

1 Maxime and Zoé have clear opinions about their work experience and they give reasons and examples to justify these opinions. Read their messages.

> J'ai fait mon stage dans un bureau. Je n'ai pas appris grand-chose parce que le patron n'avait pas beaucoup de temps pour donner des explications. Par exemple, il était toujours au téléphone. En plus, mes collègues aussi étaient toujours très occupés. **Maxime**

> Pendant mon stage au refuge, j'ai aidé à soigner les animaux, par exemple les oiseaux blessés. Je voudrais devenir vétérinaire plus tard et pour moi, c'était donc une expérience idéale. En plus, les employés étaient vraiment gentils. J'aimerais bien revenir au refuge comme bénévole l'année prochaine. **Zoé**

a An example is often introduced with *par exemple*, and a reason with *parce que*. In the texts above, circle the examples and underline the reasons given.

b Reasons don't always start with *parce que*. Note down the two common verbs which Zoé uses to say what she would like. This will help you understand her reasons and intentions, as well as her opinion.

---

2 For each writer, circle the correct opinion and justification. Note down the key words in the text in **1** that led you to your answer.

> In the second part of the sentence, there could be more than one correct answer.

a Maxime **liked / disliked** his work experience because of **the type of work / his colleagues / his future plans**.

Key words: ....

b Zoé **liked / disliked** her work experience because of **the type of work / her colleagues / her future plans**.

Key words: ....

3 Circle the correct option. Underline the key words in the text that led you to your answer.

a Je n'aime pas le travail en plein air. **Heureusement / Malheureusement**, le prof a proposé un stage dans une ferme.

b Au club de jeunes, organiser des activités sportives, **ça me plaît / ça ne me dit rien**. Je préfère les activités artistiques.

c Mathis a fait son stage dans un bureau. **Quel dommage! / Quelle chance!** Il aime beaucoup le plein air.

d Mon stage dans une cuisine était très intéressant et plus tard, **je n'ai pas envie de / j'espère** travailler comme cuisinier dans un restaurant.

Unit 7 Using deduction   53

Skills boost

3) How do I answer questions by combining information from different parts of a text?

You already know the importance of context to help you understand a text. Learn to look at a text as a whole. If you find parts of a text unclear, look for clues in the rest of it.

L'apprentissage

Après l'école, on peut devenir apprenti dans beaucoup de domaines, par exemple dans les métiers de la construction (plombier, électricien, couvreur…) mais aussi dans la restauration ou l'esthétique.

Au début, l'apprenti n'est pas beaucoup payé. Il/Elle fait sa formation professionnelle avec un patron mais doit aussi prendre des cours en CFA (Centre de formation d'apprentis).

Quand on a fini son apprentissage, on peut continuer à travailler pour un employeur. Plus tard, on peut créer sa propre entreprise, par exemple ouvrir un café ou un salon de beauté. Si on travaille dur, on peut alors bien gagner sa vie.

> Use your common sense. If *couvreur* is listed alongside *plombier* and *électricien*, it is very likely a building trade too.

> Some clues to the meaning are close to the underlined words, others further away.

1. Read the above extract from a careers advice website. Oliver underlined the text he didn't understand. Then he looked through the rest of the text for clues and circled a few things.

   a. Write ✏ the circled phrases in the table below, next to the phrases they help you to understand.

   b. Are the phrases you wrote examples (Ex), synonyms (S), antonyms (A) or explanations (Exp)? Note ✏ the correct option in the column on the right.

couvreur		
la restauration		
l'esthétique		
un patron		
CFA (Centre de formation d'apprentis)		
bien gagner sa vie		

   c. Finally, draw lines ✏ to match the French expressions on the left to the correct English equivalent on the right.

couvreur	class-based learning for apprentices
la restauration	boss, employer
l'esthétique	earn a good living
un patron	catering
CFA (Centre de formation d'apprentis)	beauty therapy
bien gagner sa vie	roofer (in the building trade)

54 Unit 7 Using deduction

Your turn!

Get back on track

Here is an exam-style question which requires you to put into practice the skills you have worked on in this unit, specifically how to use deduction to help you identify information that is not completely explicit.

Exam-style question

Le stage en entreprise

Lisez ces conseils dans le magazine *Votre avenir*.

> Un stage en entreprise peut être une très bonne expérience si on choisit bien l'entreprise. Évitez la solution de facilité, par exemple le bureau où travaillent vos parents ou le magasin à cinq minutes à pied de chez vous. Choisissez plutôt un lieu de travail qui correspond à vos projets d'avenir. Informez-vous sur l'entreprise, peut-être sur Internet, puis écrivez pour demander une place.

> Pendant un stage, on n'apprend pas grand-chose sur le travail si on prépare le café ou si on fait des photocopies toute la journée. Vous découvrirez davantage si vous bavardez avec les employés ou si vous répondez au téléphone. Parlez-vous une langue étrangère? C'est encore mieux! Pratiquez votre anglais ou votre espagnol avec les clients étrangers et vous aurez une expérience très stimulante.

1. Quel est le **meilleur** endroit pour un stage en entreprise?

   Écrivez la bonne lettre dans la case.

A	Un endroit familier
B	Un endroit intéressant
C	Un endroit facile d'accès

   (1 mark)

   > You have to identify which of the possibilities mentioned comes across as the most positive (*le meilleur* endroit). Look for more than one clue in the text in order to eliminate wrong answers.

2. Qu'est-ce que ce message recommande **exactement**?

   Écrivez la bonne lettre dans la case.

A	Parler avec les collègues et les clients
B	Aider les collègues
C	Étudier les langues

   (1 mark)

   > Again, you have to identify which option the message is most positive about. Look out for negatives and connectives on the one hand and for set phrases that give a clear positive signal on the other hand.

Unit 7 Using deduction

Your turn!

This is another exam-style question for you to try out the skills you have worked on in this unit.

Exam-style question

Mon petit boulot

Mathéo parle de son travail.

> Depuis avril, je travaille pour ma grand-mère. Je fais ses courses une fois par semaine et je passe l'aspirateur. En plus, je nettoie la salle de bains. Les travaux ménagers, ça ne me dérange pas, parce que sa maison est petite et elle me paie bien. Les courses, par contre, j'ai horreur de ça parce que j'y vais à vélo. Je suis sportif et j'adore le plein air mais malheureusement, le supermarché est très loin!
>
> De temps en temps, je promène aussi le chien de ma voisine. C'est un chien pénible qui court et qui aboie tout le temps. L'avantage, c'est que je vais au parc et c'est l'activité idéale pour moi aussi.

1. Choisissez dans la liste un aspect **positif** et un aspect **négatif** du **travail** que Mathéo fait **pour sa grand-mère**.

A	la météo
B	la distance
C	la saleté
D	la difficulté
E	l'argent

Écrivez les bonnes lettres dans les cases.

Positif ☐   Négatif ☐   (2 marks)

2. Mentionnez l'aspect **positif** du travail que Mathéo fait **pour la voisine**. Répondez en **français**.

....

(1 mark)

Start by reading options A–E, then go through the text and eliminate the options that don't apply. Remember that in a question like this, the correct answer options will normally paraphrase what is in the text.

Once you've found an option that might be correct – either a positive or a negative aspect – check for extra clues, reasons or examples to confirm your initial impression.

Negatives, connectives and some adverbs can help you recognise positive and negative attitudes. Identify one of each type in the first paragraph.

Look at the text as a whole. There is something you have learned about Mathéo in the first paragraph that could help you decide on the correct answer.

Get back on track

Review your skills

Check up

Review your response to the exam-style questions on pages 55 and 56. Tick ✓ the column to show how well you think you have done each of the following.

	Not quite ✓	Nearly there ✓	Got it! ✓
recognised positive and negative ideas	☐	☐	☐
recognised opinions and justifications	☐	☐	☐
answered questions by combining information from different parts of a text	☐	☐	☐

Need more practice?

Go back to pages 50 and 51 and do ✏️ the two exam-style questions there. Use the checklist below to help you.

Checklist Before I give my answers, have I…	✓
read the introduction to the question in order to understand the context and predict the vocabulary?	
read through the text *and* the questions?	
looked at the text as a whole to find clues for anything that's unclear?	
looked for clues to positive and negative opinions, including connectives?	
looked for reasons, examples and key phrases as clues to opinions?	

> The questions are tests, but they are not traps. Always use your common sense and, in a list of options, eliminate answers that do not make sense.

How confident do you feel about each of these **skills**? Colour in the bars.

1. How do I recognise positive and negative ideas?
2. How do I recognise opinions and justifications?
3. How do I answer questions by combining information from different parts of a text?

Unit 7 Using deduction

Get started

8 Translating accurately into English

This unit will help you learn how to translate into English accurately. The skills you will build are to:

- translate the meaning accurately
- get the tenses right
- write a clear and natural sounding translation.

In the exam, you will be asked to translate a French text of about 35–40 words into English.

It is important to know how to look out for potential difficulties and make sure you produce the best possible translation.

Read through the French text in the exam-style question below. There are some things you need to keep in mind when translating from French into English.

Do not translate the text yet. You will be asked to come back to it at the end of the unit.

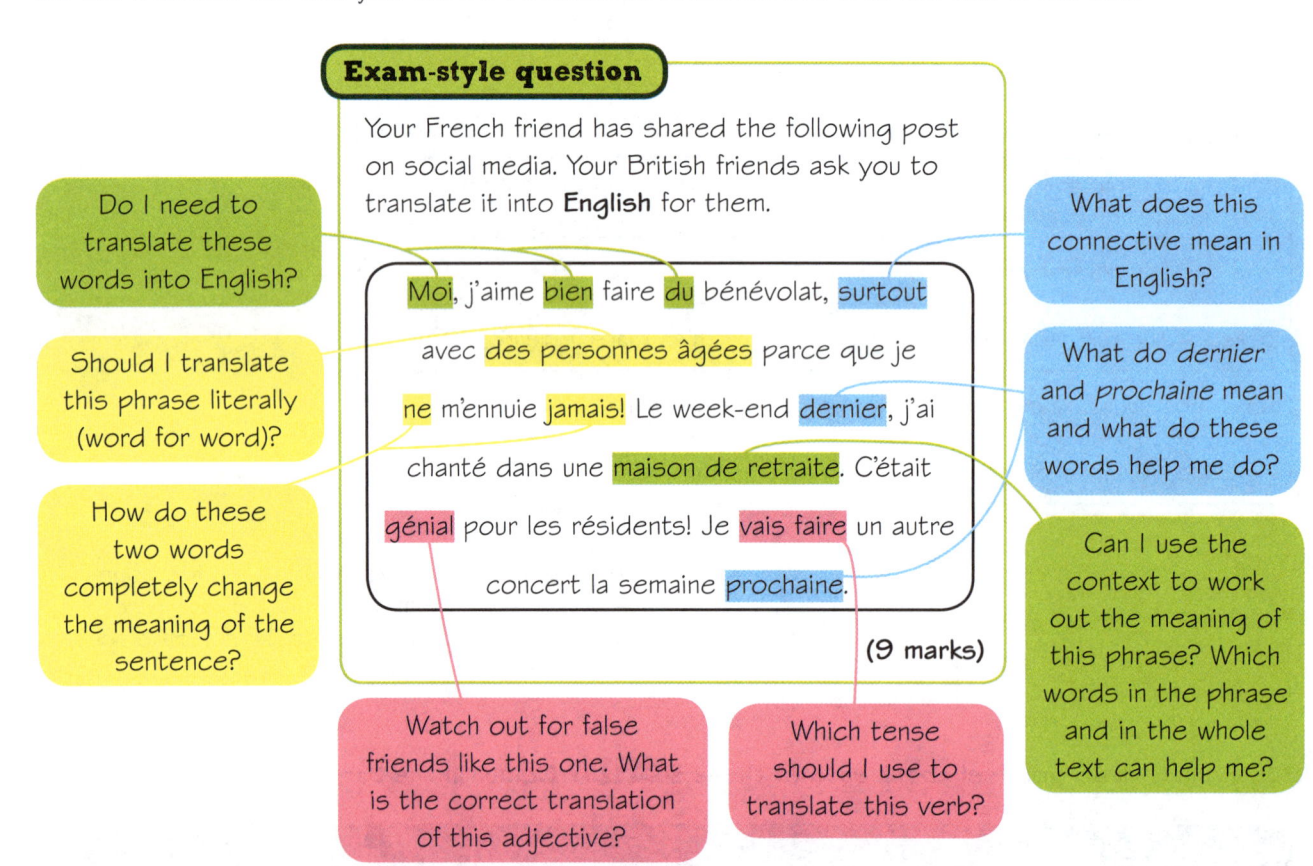

Exam-style question

Your French friend has shared the following post on social media. Your British friends ask you to translate it into **English** for them.

> Moi, j'aime bien faire du bénévolat, surtout avec des personnes âgées parce que je ne m'ennuie jamais! Le week-end dernier, j'ai chanté dans une maison de retraite. C'était génial pour les résidents! Je vais faire un autre concert la semaine prochaine.

(9 marks)

- Do I need to translate these words into English?
- Should I translate this phrase literally (word for word)?
- How do these two words completely change the meaning of the sentence?
- Watch out for false friends like this one. What is the correct translation of this adjective?
- Which tense should I use to translate this verb?
- What does this connective mean in English?
- What do *dernier* and *prochaine* mean and what do these words help me do?
- Can I use the context to work out the meaning of this phrase? Which words in the phrase and in the whole text can help me?

58   Unit 8 Translating accurately into English

Get started

Do not translate the text yet. You will be asked to come back to it at the end of the unit.

Exam-style question

Your brother's French friend has shared this post on Facebook. Your brother asks you to translate it into **English** for him.

> Moi, je ne trouve pas le jazz ennuyeux, sauf certains morceaux.
> Récemment, j'ai assisté à un concert en plein air avec mon père.
> Il faisait froid et il pleuvait mais nous nous sommes bien amusés.
> L'année prochaine, je vais y retourner avec mon frère.

(9 marks)

1 Look at a student's answer to the exam-style translation. For each sentence in the student's answer circle Ⓐ the problem or problems indicated and draw lines 🖉 to link them. One has been done for you.

a | Some words have not been translated, so the meaning is incorrect.

b | The connective has been translated incorrectly.

c | A false friend has been wrongly translated.

d | An unfamiliar phrase has been omitted. The context should help to translate it.

e | A phrase was translated too literally (word for word), which altered the meaning.

f | A phrase was translated too literally and doesn't sound natural in English.

g | The verb was translated using the wrong tense.

Student's answer:
- I find jazz annoying, (especially) certain bits.
- Recently, I assisted at a concert with my father.
- It was cold and it rained but we amused each other.
- The year next, I returned with my brother.

The three key questions in the **skills boosts** will help you to improve your translations into English.

1 How do I translate the meaning accurately?

2 How do I get the tenses right?

3 How do I write a clear and natural sounding translation?

Unit 8 Translating accurately into English   59

Skills boost

1 How do I translate the meaning accurately?

In order to translate accurately, you must:
- account for every word of the French, but do not translate any words that are not necessary in English
- pay attention to words that can change the meaning, such as negatives and connectives
- use the context to work out the meaning of unfamiliar words.

1 Read each French sentence very carefully and correct the English translation. Insert ✏️ any words that have been omitted and cross out ~~eat~~ any words which are not necessary in English.

a | Hier, ma mère a réservé une chambre avec vue sur la piscine. | Yesterday, my mother has booked a room with the swimming pool.

b | Le samedi, nous allons au marché du centre-ville à pied. | On the Saturday, we walk to the town centre on foot.

c | Lui, il ne veut plus passer les vacances en France. | Him, he wants to spend the holidays in France.

d | Je ne mange pas de viande et je ne bois jamais de boissons gazeuses. | I eat of meat and I drink of fizzy drinks.

2 Here is a French text and a translation. Write ✏️ the correct connective from the box in each gap in the translation.

On recycle tous nos déchets, **comme** le verre, et on achète toujours des produits verts, **y compris** les détergents. Je ne mange jamais de viande, **sauf** du poulet bio. J'aime tous les fruits, **surtout** les bananes.

except   like   especially   including

We recycle all our rubbish, ... glass, and we always buy green products, ... detergents. I never eat meat, ... organic chicken. I like all fruit, ... bananas.

3 The underlined word in each sentence below might be unfamiliar to you.

a Circle Ⓐ the key words in each sentence that help you understand the context.

b Choose the correct translation of each underlined word from the word box and write ✏️ it on the line.

i On se promène sur le <u>quai</u> de la rivière. ....

ii J'attends le train sur le <u>quai</u> de la gare. ....

bank   platform   quay   dock

iii J'ai de nouvelles <u>baguettes</u> pour ma batterie. ....

iv Je ne sais pas manger le riz avec des <u>baguettes</u> ....

chopsticks   wand   drumsticks   baguette

> Always look for words you recognise around an unfamiliar word or phrase.
> Try out words that make sense in the gap in your English sentence. Use your common sense!

60 Unit 8 Translating accurately into English

Skills boost

2 How do I get the tenses right?

Translating verbs using the appropriate tense can be a challenge. To help you, look out for:
- time phrases which give clues to the tense used
- the form of the verbs and the verb endings.

1 Draw lines to match each tense to the correct description and then to the correct examples.

present tense	part of *avoir* or *être* + past participle	*j'ai dansé* (I have danced/I danced) *je suis tombé(e)* (I have fallen/I fell)
perfect tense	part of *aller* + infinitive	*je vais acheter* (I'm going to buy) *je vais manger* (I'm going to eat)
imperfect tense	one word verb form with endings: e/s, e/s, e/d/t, ons, ez, ent/ont	*j'étais* (I was) *j'avais* (I had)
near future tense	one word verb form with endings: ais, ais, ait, ions, iez, aient	*je joue* (I play, I am playing) *je fais* (I do, I am doing)

2 i Underline the time phrase in each French sentence below.

ii Which time frame does each time phrase indicate? Write P for past, PR for present or F for future in the box.

iii Translate each sentence into English on paper.

a J'ai cours de maths aujourd'hui. ☐

b Demain, je vais fêter mon anniversaire. ☐

c J'ai beaucoup travaillé hier. ☐

d Le week-end dernier, je suis allé en ville. ☐

e La semaine prochaine, on va sortir. ☐

f En ce moment, j'ai trop de devoirs. ☐

g Je suis arrivée ici il y a un an. ☐

h À l'avenir, il va étudier à l'étranger. ☐

3 i Underline the verb(s) in each sentence below.

ii Label each sentence with the time frame it refers to (P, PR or F).

> The perfect tense and the near future tense both have two parts, but the two parts might not be next to each other!

iii Translate the sentences into English on paper, paying special attention to the tenses.

a Je voyage beaucoup. ☐ Je suis allé en France et c'était bien. ☐ Cet été, je vais aller en Italie. ☐

b Amir est arrivé à Paris quand il avait 7 ans. ☐ Il a appris le français et il parle très bien. ☐ Il va bientôt rentrer au collège. ☐

c Nous avons passé le week-end à la campagne. ☐ C'était nul parce qu'il n'y avait rien à faire. ☐ Nous n'allons pas y retourner. ☐

Unit 8 Translating accurately into English   **61**

Skills boost

3 How do I write a clear and natural sounding translation?

You need to be aware that you cannot translate literally from one language to another – you must find English equivalents for French idiomatic expressions.

Some French words are false friends – they look like English words but mean something different.

1 Correct each translation so that the English sounds right, including the word order.

> Translate word for word in your head first, to make sure you cover everything. How can you make the English sound natural? Don't stick too closely to the French.

a | J'ai 15 ans et je m'entends bien avec ma petite amie. | I have 15 years and I hear myself well with my little friend.

b | Je prends mon petit-déjeuner avant de partir. | I take my breakfast before to leave.

c | J'ai envie d'habiter dans une ferme isolée. | I have envy to live in a farm isolated.

d | Il y a du soleil, il fait très chaud et j'ai soif. | There is some sun, it does very hot and I have thirst.

e | Ma chambre est plus grande que la chambre de ma sœur. | My bedroom is more big than the bedroom of my sister.

2 Circle the correct translation for each word or phrase in bold.

a | Je **suis resté** sur mon **siège** toute la **journée**. | I rested / stayed on my siege / seat the whole journey / day.

b | Je n'ai pas encore **passé** tous mes examens au **collège**. | I have not yet passed / sat all my exams at college / high school.

c | Il **a eu beaucoup de chance**. Il a eu un accident **grave** mais il n'est pas **blessé**. | He was very lucky / had many chances. He had a grave / serious accident but he's not injured / blessed.

d | J'**attends** ma mère à la **librairie** quand elle **travaille**. | I attend / wait for my mother at the library / bookshop when she travels / works.

62 Unit 8 Translating accurately into English

Get back on track

Your turn!

Look at this exam-style translation task and the student's answer. Read the comments.

Exam-style question

You have received this message from your French penfriend. Translate it into **English** to show to your class.

> Ma famille et moi, nous habitons dans une ville de banlieue, tout près de Paris.
> Hier, je suis encore arrivé en retard au collège à cause de la circulation. C'est un problème grave, surtout avec tous les cars. C'est l'horreur!

(9 marks)

Not correct English — *My family and me, we live in a town, all near from Paris.* — An important word is missing.

Yesterday I arrived again late at college thanks to the circulation. — False friends

Incorrect word order — *It is a grave problem, including all the cars. It's the horror!* — Wrong translation of the connectives

False friends

This phrase cannot be translated literally. Needs an equivalent idiom.

1 Now write ✎ your own translation of the French text, following all the advice given in this unit and in the comments.

....
....
....
....
....
....
....
....
....

Unit 8 Translating accurately into English

Your turn!

Get back on track

Here is the exam-style question you saw at the start of the unit.

Exam-style question

Your French friend has sent you this email. Your parents ask you to translate it into **English** for them.

> Il y a un mois, j'ai fait un voyage scolaire à Londres. C'était génial mais je me suis cassé le pied et j'ai marché avec des béquilles. C'était énervant! Je n'ai vu que Big Ben. L'été prochain, je vais peut-être retourner à Londres.

(9 marks)

First read the whole text through in order find out the general context. Then look at each sentence, and finally at each word. (The translation text in your exam will be shorter than this one, about 35–40 words).

Think about all the things you need to be aware of. Look out for potential tricky bits: any set phrases? false friends? negatives? different word order? unfamiliar vocabulary?

1. Now write your own response to the exam-style task. Use what you have learned in this unit to help you.

Read out your finished translation (aloud or in your head). Does it sound right in English? If not, make changes so that it sounds more natural.

Unit 8 Translating accurately into English

Get back on track

Review your skills

Check up

Review your responses to the exam-style questions on pages 63 and 64. Tick ✓ the column to show how well you think you have done each of the following.

	Not quite	Nearly there	Got it!
translated the meaning accurately	☐	☐	☐
got the tenses right	☐	☐	☐
written a clear and natural sounding translation	☐	☐	☐

Need more practice?

Go back to pages 58 and 59 and answer ✎ the two exam-style questions there on paper.

Now challenge yourself to do this translation on paper. Use the checklist below to help you.

Exam-style question

Your French friend has posted this blog entry. Translate it into **English** to show your parents.

> Le samedi matin, je n'ai jamais cours mais je ne reste pas au lit car j'aide souvent mon père au magasin.
> Je n'ai qu'une sœur plus jeune, trop jeune pour aider.
> Pas de chance! Samedi dernier, j'ai quitté la maison à 5h00.
> C'était dur! Dans dix ans, je vais avoir mon propre magasin.

(9 marks)

Checklist Before I give my answers, have I …	✓
avoided translating word for word?	
worked out unfamiliar words from the context?	
checked for missing words and unnecessary words?	
translated false friends correctly?	
checked word order?	
used the correct tense?	
checked connectives and negatives?	
checked if my translation sounds natural?	

How confident do you feel about each of these **skills**? Colour ✎ in the bars.

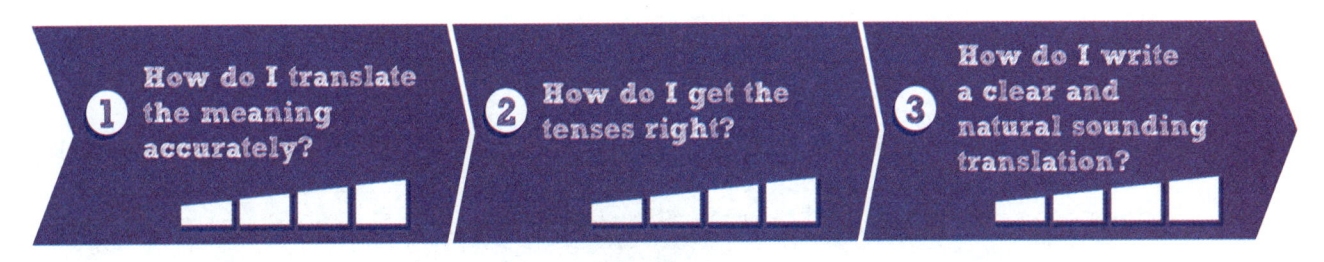

1. How do I translate the meaning accurately?
2. How do I get the tenses right?
3. How do I write a clear and natural sounding translation?

Unit 8 Translating accurately into English

Get started

9 Understanding unfamiliar language

This unit will help you with techniques to understand unfamiliar language. The skills you will build are to:

- use clues from the whole context
- use clues within the sentence, for example an explanation or a synonym
- use clues from the unfamiliar words themselves, such as similarities with more familiar words.

In the Higher exam, you will be asked to tackle reading tasks such as the ones on these two pages. This unit will prepare you to write your response to these questions.

(1) The task is headed 'Environment'. Note down five or six issues (in English if you wish), which you think could be mentioned.

global warming, ...

....

Do not answer this question yet. You will be asked to come back to it at the end of the unit.

Exam-style question

Environment

You read this blog in which Léonie shares her concerns about the environment.

> Les problèmes d'environnement nous concernent tous, même indirectement. Mes parents, par exemple, ont dû déménager. Leur maison était située en zone inondable, à côté d'une rivière qui débordait dès qu'il pleuvait. Non seulement ça, mais mon grand-père, qui est apiculteur, récolte moins de miel puisque les insectes, y compris ses abeilles, sont tués par les pesticides. Notre village est petit, et pourtant l'air est pollué parce qu'on a construit une usine trop près des habitations. De plus, les seniors comme mes grands-parents ne peuvent plus se déplacer! Il y a moins de transports en commun maintenant qu'on a réduit ou supprimé les cars et les petites lignes ferroviaires. C'est injuste et décourageant.

Complete the grids below in **English** to indicate what the problems were and why.

Example

	Problem	Reason
House	parents had to move	house at risk of flooding

1

Grandfather		

(2 marks)

2

Village		

(2 marks)

3

Older people		

(2 marks)

Underline examples and circle (near-)synonyms in the text to help you make sense of unfamiliar language.

Get started

Do not answer this question yet. You will be asked to come back to it at the end of the unit.

Exam-style question

Un e-mail

Lisez l'e-mail d'Ibtissem qui parle de ses activités extrascolaires.

De: Ibtissem@freemail.fr
Sujet: Le théâtre au collège

Salut Maxime!

Bonne nouvelle, je passe en seconde! J'ai eu un bulletin correct, avec de bonnes appréciations des professeurs (sauf pour les SVT, je trouve ça inintéressant). Pourtant, ce que j'ai le plus aimé cette année, ce ne sont pas les cours, mais les activités extrascolaires. Par exemple, on a monté une pièce de Molière, *Le Malade imaginaire*, avec la prof de français! C'était la première fois que je faisais du théâtre. C'était un vrai défi: nous avions de longues répétitions deux fois par semaine et c'était dur d'apprendre le texte, mais j'étais vraiment fière du résultat. J'avais le trac pour la première représentation, mais la prof a dit que c'était normal d'avoir peur. L'année prochaine, je vais étudier l'art dramatique au lycée!

À plus!

Ibtissem

> In the text, highlight explanations, underline examples and circle synonyms to help you make sense of unfamiliar language.

Répondez aux questions en **français**.

Exemple: Pourquoi est-ce qu'Ibtissem est contente?
Elle passe en seconde.

1 Qu'est-ce que les professeurs ont donné à Ibtissem?

   ....

   (1 mark)

2 Quelles sont les opinions d'Ibtissem sur ce qu'elle fait à l'école? Donnez **deux** détails.

   ....

   ....

   (2 marks)

3 Qu'est-ce qui était difficile avec la pièce de théâtre? Donnez **deux** détails.

   ....

   ....

   (2 marks)

4 Qu'est-ce que la prof a expliqué le jour de la représentation?

   ....

   (1 mark)

The three key questions in the **skills boosts** will help you to improve how you answer this type of question.

1. How do I use clues from the whole context?
2. How do I use clues within the sentence?
3. How do I use clues from the unfamiliar words themselves?

Unit 9 Understanding unfamiliar language   67

Skills boost

1 How do I use clues from the whole context?

You already know that the context can help you predict familiar language. It can also help you make educated guesses about unfamiliar language that you come across.

1 Read these introductions to reading questions. Circle Ⓐ and annotate ✏️ the key words.
Example:

(School) ──────────────────────────→ *main theme*
A website has published the results of an online survey on (attitudes) to (homework.)
                                                        expect opinions

a Part-time jobs
You are interested in how young people earn their pocket money.

b The environment
You are doing a project about endangered species and you find this article.

c Future plans
Read these posts by three students. They are talking about their ambitions.

d Family relationships
A French teen magazine has published an item about family relationships. Read what these girls say about their families.

e Un e-mail
Lisez l'e-mail de Nicolas qui parle de ses projets de voyage.

2 Read each short extract and underline Ⓐ the most likely meaning of the highlighted word in the context, which is given by the heading in bold. An example has been done for you.

	Vacances actives Escalade, canyoning, descente de rapides, ça c'est mon truc. J'ai horreur de **traîner** en ville et de perdre mon temps.	to train to travel <u>to hang around</u>
a	**L'environnement** Dans les bureaux des entreprises, on fait de moins en moins de photocopies parce qu'il est important de réduire son **empreinte carbone**.	fingerprint carbon footprint carbon copy
b	**Mes projets professionnels** J'aime les langues étrangères et plus tard, je voudrais **faire carrière** à l'étranger.	travel have a job visit friends
c	**Après l'école** Au lycée, je vais étudier la biologie parce que je veux devenir infirmier. Ensuite, j'irai à la fac parce que pour ce métier, il faut d'abord obtenir une **licence**.	authorisation degree permit
d	**Une sortie au théâtre** Le spectacle a commencé à 20 heures. La salle était pleine. Sur la **scène**, il y avait seulement un banc et deux hommes.	stage concert hall screen

68   **Unit 9 Understanding unfamiliar language**

Skills boost

2 How do I use clues within the sentence?

To avoid getting stuck on a word or a phrase you don't know, always look carefully at the words that come before and after as they can help you understand the unfamiliar word. For example, look out for a possible explanation or examples as well as for synonyms and antonyms.

1 Read these texts written by young people after they have finished their work placements.

a Circle (A) the correct meaning of the word in bold and underline (A) four examples in the text (one has been done).

> J'ai fait beaucoup de **tâches** ennuyeuses pendant mon stage comme faire des photocopies, coller des timbres et poster les lettres ou ranger le bureau.

tasks   errors   progress

b Circle (A) the correct meaning of the words in bold and underline (A) an explanation in the text.

> Après ce stage, je voudrais faire **une formation en alternance**, c'est-à-dire à la fois des cours au lycée professionnel et travailler dans l'entreprise.

studies   work shadowing   sandwich course

c Circle (A) the correct meaning of the word in bold and underline (A) two antonyms in the text (one has been done).

> J'ai travaillé avec une employée très **aigrie**; par contre, l'autre stagiaire était très souriante et très enthousiaste.

dynamic   bitter   helpful

d Circle (A) the correct meaning of the word in bold and underline (A) a synonym.

> J'ai adoré l'entreprise où j'ai fait mon stage. La directrice m'a dit qu'elle va m'**embaucher** pour cet été: elle va m'employer comme assistante.

to interview   to take on   to train

2 Using clues in the sentences below, work out the meaning of the bold words and write it above them. Write a letter in the box to show what kind of clue you used: explanation (E), example (Ex), synonym (S), antonym (A).

a Le festival de Cannes attire beaucoup de **vedettes**: certaines sont déjà célèbres et ont joué dans de nombreux films. Pour d'autres, c'est le premier rôle.

b La Palme d'or est le prix **décerné** au meilleur film. D'autres prix sont aussi donnés au meilleur acteur ou à la meilleure actrice, par exemple.

c En majorité, les habitants de Cannes sont **ravis**, mais certains sont mécontents car il y a trop de monde partout.

d Le président du jury est souvent un réalisateur ou une star qui a eu beaucoup de **récompenses** internationales, comme un Oscar à Hollywood, un Lion d'Or à Venise ou un Bafta à Londres.

Unit 9 Understanding unfamiliar language   69

Skills boost

3. How do I use clues from the unfamiliar words themselves?

Looking very carefully at individual words can help you understand their meaning. It is important to learn how to spot the main word within a word the (root) and to memorise the meaning of common beginnings and endings (prefixes and suffixes)

1 Look at the words in bold in these texts. Use the table to help you work out the meaning of the prefixes. On paper, write down ✏ the meaning of the words in English.

Example: *dés/ordre = dis/order (en désordre = in disorder = in a mess = untidy)*

a Le bureau était en **désordre**: j'ai dû **déplacer** tous les meubles. Il y avait des étagères **irréparables**. Les mémos de ma collègue étaient **illisibles** mais elle était **impatiente** et **mécontente** quand je ne comprenais pas. C'était **injuste** et j'étais **malheureuse**.

Prefixes	Meaning
dé-/dés-	opposite/
il-	negative/
in-/im- (+ m, b, p)	bad/
ir-	'un'-/'dis'-/
mal-	'mis'-
mé-/més- (+ vowel)	
pré-	before/pre
re-/ré-	again

b Le patron m'a dit de **refaire** du café parce qu'il voulait en **reprendre**. Après, j'ai **relu** ses mails pour corriger ses fautes et après le déjeuner, j'ai **recommencé** à **réorganiser** le bureau.

c Après le bac, je **prévois** d'étudier la **préhistoire** à l'université: je suis **prédestiné** à faire une carrière dans l'archéologie.

2 Look at the words in bold in the sentences below. Use the table underneath to help you work out the meaning of the suffix and, on paper, write down ✏ the meaning of the words in English.

Example: *appréhens/if = quality (adjective) = apprehensive*

a J'étais **appréhensif** avant mon stage mais les collègues étaient **chaleureux**.

b Moi, je voudrais travailler dans une **animalerie** ou une **biscuiterie**!

c Les qualités que j'apprécie le plus sont la **gentillesse**, la **franchise**, la **loyauté** et la **curiosité**.

d Les conditions **météorologiques** et l'activité **volcanique** et **séismique** ont des conséquences **catastrophiques**.

e Il y a une **calculette** dans la poche de ma **chemisette** dans la **camionnette**.

Suffixes	Indicating ...
-eux/-euse, -if/-ive	quality/character (adjective)
-erie	place
-é, -ié, -esse, -ise, -ité	characteristic/quality (noun)
-ique	an adjective relating to the noun form
-ette	diminutive

3 Highlight ✏ the root (the main word within the word) of each word below. Then work out the meaning of each word and write ✏ it down.

Example: ir==respect==ueux = disrespectful

a inamical ....
b refroidissement ....
c agrandir..
d enregistrer ....
e décourageant ....

70 **Unit 9 Understanding unfamiliar language**

Your turn!

Get back on track

Here is an exam-style question which requires you to put into practice the skills you have worked on, specifically how to make use of the general context and the words around unfamiliar words.

> **Top tips to help you understand unfamiliar words**
> - Use the context: look for clues in the heading or in the instructions as well as illustrations, if any.
> - Look for clues in the sentence, for example an explanation of the unfamiliar word. Look for commas, brackets or dashes that introduce the explanation.
> - Look for synonyms and antonyms of the unfamiliar word. Look out for contrasting phrases like *mais* and *par contre* which may introduce antonyms.
> - Look for the phrases *par exemple* or *comme* that introduce examples to illustrate the word you don't know.

Exam-style question

World of work

You read this blog about a disastrous first part-time job.

> Mon premier boulot, c'était serveur. J'ai détesté l'ambiance du restaurant car les serveurs n'étaient pas accueillants, ils étaient même désagréables avec les clients.
>
> Au début, le patron était furieux parce que j'étais très maladroit: je cassais beaucoup de vaisselle, comme des assiettes et des verres. Alors, il m'a demandé de préparer des cocktails au bar.
>
> Seulement voilà, comme je ne connaissais rien aux alcools, les clients refusaient de boire mes cocktails, ils étaient imbuvables!
>
> Et puis j'étais très mal payé vu que je n'avais pas les pourboires (la monnaie que les clients laissaient sur la table pour moi). Le patron était malhonnête – il gardait tout l'argent.

Complete the tables below in **English** to indicate what the problems were and why.

Example

	Problem	Reason
restaurant	bad atmosphere	unpleasant staff

1

	Problem	Reason
at the beginning		

(2 marks)

2

	Problem	Reason
work at the bar		

(2 marks)

3

	Problem	Reason
wages		

(2 marks)

Unit 9 Understanding unfamiliar language

Get back on track

Your turn!

This is another exam-style question for you to try out the skills you have worked on in this unit.

> **Exam-style question**
>
> Un e-mail
>
> Lisez l'e-mail de Ravi, un jeune francophone de Pondichéri en Inde, qui parle de la fête de Diwali.
>
> | De: Ravi359@hotmail.com |
> | --- |
> | Sujet: La grande fête de Diwali |
>
> Diwali approche, j'ai très hâte de le fêter! J'ai des souvenirs inoubliables, vraiment précieux, de cette fête quand j'étais petit… tellement j'avais plaisir à retrouver toute ma famille.
>
> Un ou deux jours avant la fête, les gens nettoient leurs maisons et les décorent avec des bougies. Ma mère était très intransigeante sur la propreté, elle voulait une maison très nette pour impressionner ses invités qui étaient nombreux!
>
> Nos visiteurs m'apportaient tous des pochettes de bonbons et de petits gâteaux. J'en mangeais pendant des semaines! C'est sans doute de là que date ma gourmandise: j'adore les sucreries!
>
> Selon la tradition, ma grand-mère me faisait toujours des vêtements neufs pour Diwali mais ils étaient immettables, beaucoup trop grands! Pourtant ma mère m'obligeait à les porter par politesse envers ma grand-mère. C'est mon seul mauvais souvenir de cette fête!
>
> Répondez aux questions en **français**.
>
> **Exemple**: Ravi est impatient. Pourquoi?
>
> *C'est bientôt Diwali.*
>
> 1 Pourquoi Ravi se souvient-il des fêtes de Diwali quand il était petit?
>
> ....
>
> (1 mark)
>
> 2 Qu'est-ce qui était important pour la mère de Ravi? Pourquoi? Donnez **deux** détails.
>
> ....
>
> ....
>
> (2 marks)
>
> 3 Pourquoi Ravi aime-t-il les choses sucrées?
>
> ....
>
> (1 mark)
>
> 4 Pourquoi Ravi n'aimait-il pas porter des habits neufs pour Diwali? Donnez **deux** détails.
>
> ....
>
> ....
>
> (2 marks)

> Revise the advice on page 46 about giving the right amount of detail when lifting answers from a French text.

Get back on track

Review your skills

Check up

Review your response to the exam-style questions on pages 71 and 72. Tick ✓ the column to show how well you think you have done each of the following.

	Not quite ✓	Nearly there ✓	Got it! ✓
used clues from the whole context	☐	☐	☐
used clues within the sentence, for example an explanation or a synonym	☐	☐	☐
used clues from the unfamiliar words themselves	☐	☐	☐

Need more practice?

Go back to pages 66 and 67 and do ✎ the two exam-style questions there. Use the checklist below to help you.

Checklist Before I give my answers, have I …	✓
read the introduction to the question in order to understand the context and predict the vocabulary?	☐
read through the text *and* the questions?	☐
used what I know about the context to have an educated guess at unfamiliar vocabulary?	☐
looked for clues to unfamiliar vocabulary within a sentence, such as synonyms/antonyms, examples, explanations?	☐
tried to understand unfamiliar words by identifying common beginnings and endings?	☐
tried to understand unfamiliar words by identifying the root (the main word within a word)?	☐

- Use your knowledge of French, but also your common sense: the answers won't always be obvious, but they will be realistic.
- In an exam situation, focus on answering the questions. Don't worry about unfamiliar language in the text if it's definitely not needed to answer the questions.

How confident do you feel about each of these **skills**? Colour ✎ in the bars.

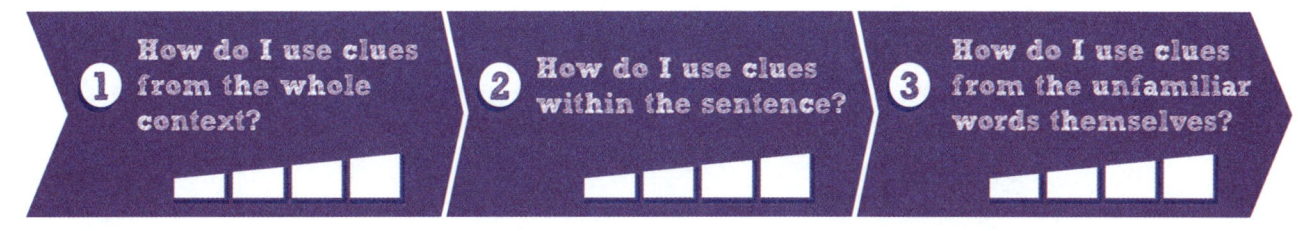

1. How do I use clues from the whole context?
2. How do I use clues within the sentence?
3. How do I use clues from the unfamiliar words themselves?

Unit 9 Understanding unfamiliar language 73

Answers

Unit 1

Page 3

1) Sample answer

   A *le match de foot, le joueur, le ballon, le stade, le but, jouer, gagner, perdre*

   B *le cinéma, le film, l'acteur, l'histoire, triste, amusant*

   C *le magasin, la boutique, le centre commercial, les vêtements, les chaussures, les jeux vidéo, cher, pas cher*

   D *le bowling, la boule, jouer, jeter, gagner, perdre*

   E *le cirque, le clown, l'acrobate, les musiciens*

Page 4

1) Ac, Bd, Cc, Da, Eb

Page 5

1) A P
   B PN
   C N
   D PN

2) nous avons les mêmes – we've got the same

   il aime – he likes

   je préfère – I prefer

   nous adorons – we love

   elle écoute mes secrets – she listens to my secrets

   elle ne les répète pas – she doesn't repeat them

3) a all the same – *quand même*
   b but (also) – *mais (aussi)*
   c by contrast – *par contre*
   d moreover – *en plus*
   e not always – *pas toujours*
   f unfortunately – *malheureusement*

4) A P: *nous avons les mêmes centres d'intérêt; nous adorons tous les deux le foot; il est fidèle et généreux*

   B P: *très sympa; elle écoute mes secrets mais elle ne les répète pas; vraiment gentille*

   N: *pas toujours très patiente*

   PN: *indépendante*

   C P: *intelligent*

   N: *impatient; agaçant; arrogant*

   D P: *très amusante; marrant; je l'aime bien*

   N: *têtue et pas très sensible*

Page 6

1) a Circle: wife, fishing, loud, nine
   b Circle: town hall. Underline: *ville*

   Circle: coffee. Underline: *boisson*

   Circle: strong. Underline: *je préfère le coca*

   Circle: menu. Underline: *pizza pescatore*

   Circle: own. Underline: *je voudrais avoir*

   Circle: expensive. Underline: *beaucoup d'argent*

2) a V – He is wearing a jumper.
   b N – It's the front door.
   c N – She sleeps in a big bed.
   d V – She's reading a magazine.
   e PP – She came back at 7pm.
   f N – School starts again on September 3rd.
   g V – He runs fast.
   h A – My trousers are short.
   i N – I saw a play.
   j N – I've got a one-euro coin.

Page 7

1) Circle: *excellente, tristes, riche, modeste célèbre, hyper-célèbre, clair courageuse, travailleuse, intelligente*

2) Highlight: *Mais, toujours, De plus, mais, quand même Certainement, parce que, beaucoup énormément, juste, mais, très, En plus*

Exam-style question

1 Léa PN

2 Ali N

3 Pauline P

Page 8

Exam-style question

1 B, 2 D, 3 E, 4 A

Page 9

Page 2 exam-style question

1 Maelys P

2 Mohamed PN

3 Adrien PN

Page 3 exam-style question

1 E, 2 A, 3 C, 4 B

Unit 2

Page 11

1 a Underline:

cognates: passion, tour, champion, million, super

near-cognates: participer, cycliste, crabes, coûte

b Circle: grand, passe

Page 12

2 a Underline: impossible, concept, original, reporter, talent, culture, tradition, importance, sofa, expérience, films, science-fiction, simple, impact, public

b A It's impossible to be bored during this programme: the concept is very original, the reporter has talent and with him, culture becomes fascinating!

B We had a family tradition which was very important (which had great importance) when I was little: on Saturday nights, we could eat on the sofa and watch a series on TV! What an experience!

C I really appreciate the old black and white science-fiction films: the story/plot was very simple but they had a lot of impact on the public in the fifties.

3 Sample answers

-al	-ance	-ence	-ent	-ble	-ct	-tion
central	distance	patience	urgent	horrible	correct	attention
animal	arrogance	violence	agent	invisible	abject	action
idéal	ambulance	expérience	décent	flexible	exact	audition
mental	tolérance	intelligence	content	adorable	direct	solution
spécial	finance	absence	clément	excitable	respect	éducation
etc.	etc.	etc.	etc.	etc.	etc.	etc.

Page 13

1 a i Highlight: spectateurs, sûrement, apprécier, monstre, film (5)

ii Highlight: documentaire, relativement, sérieux, amusant, comique (5)

iii Highlight: actif, sport, individuel (3)

iv Highlight: futur, tourisme, espace, aventure, inimaginable (5)

v Highlight: historiques, étranges, mystère (3)

vi Highlight: honnête, employeur, approuver, sens, humour (5)

vii Highlight: journaliste, commentaire, visite, officielle, ministre (5)

viii Highlight: préfère, réalité, virtuelle, social, compagnie (5)

ix Highlight: problèmes, techniques, découragé, inventé, cinéma (5)

b i The spectators will surely appreciate the monster in this film.

ii This documentary is relatively serious but also very funny and sometimes comical.

iii I'm very active and I do an individual sport.

iv Pastimes of the future? Space tourism, an unimaginable adventure!

v These old historic buildings are a little strange and full of mystery.

vi To be honest, the employer won't approve of your sense of humour.

vii The journalist is giving a commentary on the minister's official visit.

viii He prefers the virtual reality of a social network to the company of his friends.

ix Technical problems didn't discourage the Lumière brothers when they invented cinema.

2

French	English	Examples from sentences
nouns		
consonant	add –e	futur/future, sens/sense
-e	remove –e	visite/visit, problèmes/problems
-el/-é -i/-ie	-y	mystère/mystery, réalité/reality
-re	-er	monstre/monster, ministre/minister
nouns or adjectives		
-iste/-isme	-ist/-ism	tourisme/tourism, journaliste/journalist
-aire	-ary	documentaire/documentary, commentaire/commentary
-el(le)	-al	individuel/individual, officielle/official, virtuelle/virtual
-que	-c/-ck/-k/-cal	comique/comical, historique/historic, technique/technical
adverbs		
-(e)ment	-ly	sûrement/surely, relativement/relatively

Page 14

1 a, b

False friends	Incorrect translation	Correct translation
attends	am attending	am waiting for
en retard	on retard	late
journée	journey	day
marche	marches	walks
pain	pain	bread
bras	bras	arms
crie	cries	shouts
veste	vest	jacket
marron	maroon	brown
grande	grand	big
gros	gross	fat
boutons	buttons	pimples
figure	figure	face
sympathique	sympathetic	nice
de location	on location	for hire
car	car	coach
propre	proper	clean

demande	demands	asks
parfum	perfume	flavour
gentil	gentle	kind
reste	rest	stay
banc	bank	bench
pins	pins	pines
joli	jolly	pretty
chat	chat	cat

2
- a at the moment
- b injured
- c the occasion/opportunity/luck
- d high school
- e bookshop
- f change/currency
- g second-hand
- h to sit an exam
- i meeting

Page 15

Exam-style question

C, E

Page 16

Exam-style question

1 Morgane, 2 Katya, 3 Chloé 4 Mathieu

Page 17

Page 10 exam-style question

1 Katia, 2 Tristan, 3 Étienne, 4 Josy

Page 11 exam-style question

B, D

Unit 3

Page 19

1 Sample answer

birthday party, Mother's / Father's Day, school prom, Christmas, New Year's Eve, Hanukkah, Eid

Page 20

1
- a au collège – à l'école – to school
- b copains – amis – friends
- c j'adore – j'aime beaucoup – I love
- d une galette – un gâteau – cake
- e très intéressante – passionnant – very interesting / exciting / fascinating
- f j'ai horreur de – je déteste – I hate

2
- a de bonne heure – tôt
- b prends – mange
- c à bicyclette – à vélo
- d un blouson – une veste
- e au gymnase – à la salle de sport
- f férié – de fête
- g un billet – un ticket
- h contente – heureuse

Page 21

1 a, b

super	great	nul	rubbish
d'avantages	advantages	d'inconvénients	disadvantages
fatigant	tiring	reposant	restful
paresseuse	lazy	active	active
j'aime bien	I like	je déteste	I dislike / hate
cher	expensive	bon marché	cheap
mauvaise	bad	bonne	good
ouverts	open	fermés	closed
se reposer	to rest	travailler	to work

2 i a True
  b True
  c False – The shops in the shopping centre are not expensive.
  d True
  e False – He is annoyed with the price he paid.

ii Mes tennis sont très vieilles et aussi trop petites (a). Je suis allé en ville pour acheter de nouvelles chaussures, d'une pointure plus grande (a). J'habite loin (b) du centre commercial, donc je suis allé dans une boutique en ville. Les magasins du centre commercial sont bon marché (c), c'est vrai, mais en ville, c'est plus (b) près pour moi.

Dans la boutique, j'ai essayé une paire de tennis pas chères mais vraiment démodées (d)... Je n'étais pas content, alors le vendeur a apporté une autre paire, très à la mode (d).

J'ai payé les chaussures 120 euros! C'est très cher (c) et ça m'énerve (e), mais je suis heureux (e) d'avoir une belle paire de tennis.

Page 22

1 Ah, Bb, Ce, Df, Ec, Fd, Ga, Hg

2
- a vert
- b plat
- c fête
- d magasin
- e sucré
- f fêter
- g détester
- h ordre
- i marrant
- j cher
- k d'habitude
- l quelquefois

Page 23

1 Circle:
- a pâtisseries, gâteaux, beignets
- b cousins, membres de la famille
- c offre, donne

Exam-style question

1. Playing with children — 3
2. Lots of light — 2
3. Eating sweet food — 1
4. Receiving presents — 5

Page 24

1 Circle:
- a détendre
- b stressant
- c tard
- d me reposer, me détendre
- e Je range, je nettoie la salle de bains, je lave la voiture …

Exam-style question

1. Antoine — B
2. Khadija — A
3. Clément — D

Page 25

Page 18 exam-style question

1. Helping at home — 5
2. Using public transport — 1
3. Relaxing — 4
4. Studying — 3

Page 19 exam-style question

1. Amir — C
2. Léa — E
3. Justine — B

Unit 4

Page 28

1 Aj, Ba, Ce, Dg, Ef, Fd, Gi, Hb, Ih, Jc

2
- a Circle: A combien, B Où, C Qui, D Qu'est-ce que, E Comment, F Est-ce que, G Quand, H Depuis quand, I Quel, J Pourquoi
- b Ag, Bi, Cb, Dj, Ed, Fc, Gh, He, Ia, Jf

Page 29

1
- a before
  - How far Hennebont is from the sea = about 15 kilometres
  - The kind of town it is = historic and touristy
- b after
  - How long Yannick has lived there = all his life
  - An attraction for animal lovers = the horse museum
- c before
  - Jis favourite feature of Hennebont = the river
  - Jis reason for liking the river = he likes kayaking
- d before
  - His favourite sport = swimming
  - A pastime he does with his brother = sea fishing

2
- a Bretagne (Brittany)
- b Normandie (Normandy)
- c non, une région voisine (no, it's a neighbouring region)
- d au centre-ville (town centre)
- e de temps en temps (from time to time)

Page 30

1 Circle:
- A températures, remonter, agréable
- B parapluie: umbrella
- C tout va être blanc: everything will be white
- D nuageuse: cloudy, nous allons voir le soleil: we'll see the sun
- E on ne va pas du tout voir le soleil: we won't see the sun at all
- F températures, plus fraîches: temperatures, cooler

2 a i, b ii, c iii, d ii, e i, f iii

3
- a Circle:
  - i habitants, sympathiques, avec les visiteurs
  - ii intéressants, pas ordinaires
  - iii 56 étages, la vue
  - iv petites maisons individuelles
- b quirky: b; detached houses: d, skyscrapers: c, welcoming: a

Page 31

Exam-style question

1 A, 2 B, 3 D, 4 D, 5 C

Page 32

Exam-style question

1 B
2 by creating a music festival (in the castle)
3 A
4 introduce electric shuttles/buses

Page 33

Page 26 exam-style question

1 C
2 D
3 B
4 C
5 B

Page 27 exam-style question

1 B,
2 the rubbish on the streets and in the parks
3 B

Unit 5

Page 35

1 Émilien, Marc

Page 36

1
- a Moi aussi, j'ai un vélo.
- b Je fais du vélo en vacances.
- c Cet été, je vais en Espagne.
- d J'emporte mon vélo et Sophie emporte sa planche à voile.
- e Sophie et moi, on adore le plein air!

2 Le soir, je rentre au camping, **je** prends une douche, on **dîne** vers 19 heures, puis je **retrouve** mes amis au café.

Quelquefois, on **retourne** à la plage après le dîner et **mon copain Jules** joue de la guitare. S'il **fait** chaud, on **prend** un bain de minuit.]

3 The English equivalent is 'that'
- a Je pense que la planche à voile, c'est très amusant.
- b Elle dit qu'elle veut retourner en Espagne.
- c Il déclare qu'il n'aime pas le vélo.
- d Je trouve que les vacances sont trop courtes.

Page 37

1 Hier, il a plu toute la journée. J'ai reçu un message de Sophie. J'ai mis un chapeau, j'ai pris un parapluie et on a bu un chocolat chaud au café. Ensuite, on a lu le journal, puis on a vu un film au cinéma.

2
- a Younes est monté à la tour Eiffel et il a dit «Elle est haute!»
- b Romain est gentil, il s'est levé à 7 heures et il a aidé sa mère.
- c Sara a fini la course cycliste à 14h30. Elle est rapide, elle est arrivée première.

3

je	tu	il/elle/on	nous	vous	ils/elles
-ais	-ais	-ait	-ions	-iez	-aient

4
- a Le week-end, je vais à la piscine. Samedi, pour changer, je vais jouer au tennis.
- b Tu vas au bord de la mer avec Tom? Vous allez faire de la planche à voile?
- c Mes sœurs vont en ville parce qu'elles vont retrouver des copines.
- d Tu vas faire du camping cet été? – Oui, je vais acheter une tente aujourd'hui.

Page 38

1 a, b

Madame Dubois va se détendre au bord de la mer avec ses enfants, Jules et Aglaé: | F | P |

"Aglaé, tu vas t'occuper du chien!" | F | P |

"Les enfants, vous n'allez pas vous chamailler!" | F | N |

Alors, est-ce que Madame Dubois s'est bien reposée à la plage? | Perf | Q |

Non, parce que Jules et Aglaé ne s'entendent pas du tout: | Pr | N |

"Aglaé, tu ne t'es pas promenée avec le chien!" | Perf | N |

"Et toi, Jules, tu ne te laves jamais!" | Pr | N |

Ils se sont disputés toute la journée. | Perf | P |

2 Quand j'étais à Paris, j'ai perdu mon porte-monnaie. J'ai vu un agent de police et je **lui** ai parlé. Il **m'**a demandé: «Où l'as-tu laissé?» J'ai dit que je l'ai oublié dans le métro. Je **lui** ai donné mon numéro de téléphone et l'agent **m'**a dit: «Le bureau des objets trouvés va **t'**appeler.» Je l'ai remercié… mais le bureau ne **m'**a jamais appelée. J'ai alors téléphoné à ma mère et je **lui** ai expliqué le problème. «Je vais **t'**envoyer de l'argent», a-t-elle dit. Merci Maman!

Page 39

Exam-style question

1 45%

2 77%

3 63%

4 They used to go camping when they were younger but they now prefer staying in hotels.

Page 40

Exam-style question

1 one month

2 4 a.m.

3 4

4 he didn't like it as much as his time in Arcachon

Page 41

Page 34 exam-style question

1 58%

2 40%

3 8%

4 they used to go to other seaside towns but they can relax better in Biarritz because it's quieter

Page 35 exam-style question

1 admire him on his windsurf

2 it is very cold

3 the club

4 very nice

Unit 6

Page 42

1 pourquoi = why

Sample question words: qu'est-ce que … / est-ce que … / où / qui / combien (de) / quand / comment / depuis quand / quel / quelle / quels / quelles + noun

78 Answers

Page 43

2
1. Why doesn't Lucas do a lot of sport?
2. Why doesn't he always go to basketball training?
3. What does he do in order not to put on weight?
4. What would he like to do in the future in order to keep fit?

Page 44

1
a) Why didn't Alina go on the school trip with her class?
   - i because they went to France: wrong, as that's not the reason
   - ii because she was disappointed: wrong, it's the consequence of her not going, not the cause
   - iii because she loves travelling with her class: wrong answer, doesn't make sense
   - iv because she was ill: correct answer

b) How does Théo go to school when it's not raining?
   - i on foot: wrong, he walks when the weather is fine
   - ii in order to chat with his friends: wrong, doesn't answer the question
   - iii twenty minutes: wrong, doesn't answer the question
   - iv by car: correct answer

Page 45

1
a)
   - i How did Zoé's parents reward her good marks?
   - ii What did she like during the school trip?
   - iii What was the objective of the sports tournament?
   - iv How do we know that Zoé is very sporty?

b)
   - i ils lui ont donné 50 euros (d'argent de poche)
   - ii add: elle a fait de gros progrès en espagnol.
   - iii récolter de l'argent pour une association humanitaire
   - iv add: elle a gagné tous ses matchs!

Page 46

1 Je trouve mon école très sympa. C'est un établissement privé pour garçons, [A] dans la banlieue de Montréal [B]. Notre journée commence à 8h30 et finit à 16h30. Nous avons des cours de 45 minutes [C] et deux récréations d'un quart d'heure. Pendant la pause déjeuner qui dure une heure trente, je discute avec mes copains en mangeant à la cantine [D] et on s'amuse à jouer un peu au foot dans la cour [D]. L'après-midi, je suis fatigué mais après les cours, je vais aux répétitions de la chorale de l'école [E] et je fais mes devoirs.

2
a) aux États-Unis ~~au mois de juillet~~ : the month is irrelevant to the question / the question asks for the country not when

b) son père a un nouveau travail à New York, ~~une ville très intéressante~~ : the question asks why she's going there, and it is because of her dad's job not because the town is interesting

c) il est très strict ~~mais les profs sont sympa~~ : the question is about the school not the teachers

3
A un établissement privé pour garçons
B dans la banlieue de Montréal
C 45 minutes
D il discute avec ses copains + il joue un peu au foot
E il fait partie de la chorale / il va aux répétitions de la chorale

Page 47

Exam-style question

1 D
2 elle n'était plus avec ses amies

Page 48

Exam-style question

1 pendant deux semaines
2 long: Kevin habitait assez loin
3 pratique (parce que c'était facile de choisir les vêtements le matin) et aussi très égalitaire
4 manger un pique-nique dans une boîte et quitter l'école à trois heures et demie

Page 49

Page 42 exam-style question

1 A
2 il y a du choix

Page 43 exam-style question

1 (il n'a) pas beaucoup de temps
2 il doit aider sa mère à / il doit faire les courses
3 jamais de frites + évite les desserts et les bonbons
4 devenir végétarien + s'inscrire à un club de gym

Unit 7

Page 51

1 Tick: **a**

Page 52

1 and **2**

Circle: pas bien payé (N), bon (P), fatigant (N), pas difficile (P), ennuyeux (N), fatigué (N), pas agréable (N)

3
a)
i	j'adore ça	P
ii	je trouve ça …	PN
iii	on est obligé de …	N
iv	j'ai gagné beaucoup d'argent	P
v	l'avantage, c'est que …	P

b)
	ça va	P
	avoir toujours les mains dans l'eau froide	N

4 a par conséquent — R
   b en plus — R
   c personnellement — DD
   d par contre — DD
   e donc — R
   f mais — DD

Page 53

1 a J'ai fait mon stage dans un bureau. Je n'ai pas appris grand-chose <u>parce que le patron n'avait pas beaucoup de temps pour donner des explications</u>. <u>Par exemple, il était toujours au téléphone</u>. En plus, mes collègues aussi étaient toujours très occupés. **Maxime**

   Pendant mon stage au refuge, j'ai aidé à soigner les animaux, <u>par exemple les oiseaux blessés</u>. Je voudrais devenir vétérinaire plus tard et pour moi, c'était donc une expérience idéale. En plus, les employés étaient vraiment gentils. J'aimerais bien revenir au refuge comme bénévole l'année prochaine. **Zoé**

   b je voudrais, j'aimerais

2 a Maxime ~~liked~~ / **disliked** his work experience because of ~~the type of work~~ / **his colleagues** / ~~his future plans~~.

   Key words: pas appris grand-chose, le patron n'avait pas beaucoup de temps, toujours au téléphone, collègues… très occupés

   b Zoé **liked** / ~~disliked~~ her work experience because of **the type of work** / **her colleagues** / **her future plans**.

   Key words: Je voudrais devenir vétérinaire, une expérience idéale, vraiment gentils, j'aimerais bien revenir

3 a <u>Je n'aime pas le travail en plein air</u>. ~~Heureusement~~ / **Malheureusement**, le prof a proposé un stage <u>dans une ferme</u>.

   b Au club de jeunes, organiser des activités <u>sportives</u>, ~~ça me plaît~~ / **ça ne me dit rien**. Je préfère les activités <u>artistiques</u>.

   c Mathis a fait son stage dans <u>un bureau</u>. **Quel dommage!** / ~~Quelle chance!~~ Il aime beaucoup <u>le plein air</u>.

   d Mon stage dans une <u>cuisine</u> était <u>très intéressant</u> et plus tard, **j'espère** / ~~je n'ai pas envie de~~ travailler comme <u>cuisinier dans un restaurant</u>.

Page 54

1 a, b

couvreur	les métiers de la construction	Ex
la restauration	un café	Ex
l'esthétique	un salon de beauté	Ex
un patron	pour un employeur	S
CFA (Centre de formation d'apprentis)	prendre des cours	Exp
bien gagner sa vie	pas beaucoup payé	A

c couvreur – roofer (in the building trade)

la restauration – catering

l'esthétique – beauty therapy

un patron – boss, employer

CFA (Centre de formation d'apprentis) – class-based learning for apprentices

bien gagner sa vie – earn a good living

Page 55

Exam-style question

1 B
2 A

Page 56

Exam-style question

1 Positif — E
   Négatif — B

2 Il va au parc et c'est l'activité idéale pour lui.

Page 57

Page 50 exam-style question

1 B
2 A

Page 51 exam-style question

1 Positif — D
   Négatif — C

2 la langue, parce que Mariana parle un peu l'espagnol

Unit 8

Page 59

1 a I **find** jazz annoying, **especially** certain bits.

   Recently, I **assisted at** **a concert** with my father.

   It was cold and it rained but **we amused each** other.

   The year next, I **returned** with my brother.

Page 60

1 a Yesterday, my mother ~~has~~ booked a room with **a view of** the swimming pool.

   b On ~~the~~ Saturday~~s~~, we walk to **the market in** the town centre ~~on foot~~. /

   On ~~the~~ Saturday~~s~~, we ~~walk~~ **go** to **the market in** the town centre ~~on foot~~.

   c ~~Him,~~ he **no longer** wants to spend the holidays in France. /

   ~~Him,~~ he **doesn't** wants to spend the holidays in France **any more**.

   d I **don't** eat ~~of~~ meat and I **never** drink ~~of~~ fizzy drinks.

② Correct order: including, like, except, especially

③ a Circle: **i** rivière, **ii** train, gare, **iii** batterie, **iv** manger, riz

   b **i** bank, **ii** platform, **iii** drumsticks, **iv** chopsticks

Page 61

①

present tense	one word verb form with endings: e/s, e/s, e/d/t, ons, ez, ent/ont	je joue (I play, I am playing)
		je fais (I do, I am doing)
perfect tense	part of *avoir* or *être* + past participle	j'ai dansé (I have danced/I danced)
		je suis tombé(e) (I have fallen/I fell)
imperfect tense	one word verb form with endings: ais, ais, ait, ions, iez, aient	j'étais (I was)
		j'avais (I had)
near future tense	part of *aller* + infinitive	je vais acheter (I'm going to buy)
		je vais manger (I'm going to eat)

② i, ii, iii

a J'ai cours de maths <u>aujourd'hui</u>. [PR]
   I've got a maths lesson today.

b <u>Demain</u>, je vais fêter mon anniversaire. [F]
   Tomorrow, I'm going to celebrate my birthday.

c J'ai beaucoup travaillé <u>hier</u>. [P]
   I worked a lot yesterday.

d <u>Le week-end dernier</u>, je suis allé en ville. [P]
   Last weekend, I went to / into town.

e <u>La semaine prochaine</u>, on va sortir. [F]
   Next week, we are going to go out.

f <u>En ce moment</u>, j'ai trop de devoirs. [PR]
   At the moment, I have too much homework.

g Je suis arrivée ici <u>il y a un an</u>. [P]
   I arrived here a year ago.

h <u>À l'avenir</u>, il va étudier à l'étranger. [F]
   In the future/Later on, he's going to study abroad.

③ i, ii, iii

a Je <u>voyage</u> beaucoup. [Pr] Je <u>suis allé</u> en France et <u>c'était</u> bien. [P] Cet été, je <u>vais aller</u> en Italie. [F]
   I travel a lot. I went to France and it was good. This summer, I'm going (to go) to italy.

b Amir <u>est arrivé</u> à Paris quand il <u>avait</u> 7 ans. [P] Il <u>a appris</u> le français et il <u>parle</u> très bien. [P + Pr] Il va bientôt <u>rentrer</u> au collège. [F]
   Amir arrived in Paris when he was 7. He (has) learned French and he speaks very well. He is soon going to go to secondary school.

c Nous <u>avons passé</u> le week-end à la campagne. [P] C'était nul parce qu'il n'y <u>avait</u> rien à faire. [P] Nous n'<u>allons</u> pas y <u>retourner</u>. [F]
   We spent the weekend in the countryside. It was rubbish because there was nothing to do. We won't go back there.

Page 62

① a I am 15 (years old) and I get on well with my girlfriend.

   b I have my breakfast before leaving.

   c I feel like living / I'd like to live on an isolated farm.

   d It' sunny, it's very hot and I am thirsty

   e My bedroom is bigger than my sister's (bedroom).

② a Circle: stayed, seat, day

   b Circle: sat, high school

   c Circle: was very lucky, serious, injured

   d Circle: wait for, bookshop, works

Page 63

Exam-style question

<u>My family and I</u> live in a town <u>in the suburbs</u>, <u>very near</u> Paris.

Yesterday I arrived at <u>school</u> <u>late again</u> <u>because of</u> the <u>traffic</u>.

It is a <u>serious</u> problem, <u>especially</u> with all the <u>coaches</u>. It's <u>horrible</u> / <u>a nightmare</u>!

Page 64

Exam-style question

A month ago,
(not : There is a month)
I went on a school trip to London.
(not: I did a school trip)
It was great
(not: genial)
except I broke my foot
(not i broke myself a foot)
and I walked on crutches.
It was annoying!
(not unnerving)
I only saw Big Ben.
(not: I didn't see)
Next summer
(not: The summer next)
I'm perhaps going to go back to London.
(remember to include the adverb)

Page 65

Page 58 exam-style question

I like doing voluntary work, especially with elderly people because I never get bored! Last weekend, I sang in a retirement home. It was great for the residents! I am going to give/do another concert next week.

Page 59 exam-style question

I don't find jazz boring, except certain pieces. Recently, I attended/went to an open air concert with my father/dad. It was cold and it was raining but we had fun/enjoyed ourselves. Next year, I'm going to go back (there) with my brother.

Exam-style question

(On) Saturday mornings, I never have lessons/classes but I don't stay in bed because I often help my father/dad in the shop.

I only have one younger sister, too young to help. Bad luck!

Last Saturday, I left home at 5am. It was hard! In ten years' time, I will have my own shop.

Unit 9

Page 68

1. Sample answer

   a. (Part-time jobs) — main theme

   You are interested in how young people (earn) their (pocket money.) — main theme

   b. The environment

   You are doing a project about (endangered species) and you find this article. — main theme

   c. (Future plans) — main theme; expect future tense and conditional

   Read these posts by three students. They are talking about their (ambitions.) — main theme; expect future tense and conditional

   d. Family relationships

   A French teen magazine has published an item about (family relationships.) — main theme

   Read what these girls say about their families.

   e. Un e-mail

   Lisez l'e-mail de Nicolas qui parle de ses projets de (voyage.) — main theme; expect future tense and conditional

2. Underline:
   a. carbon footprint
   b. have a job
   c. degree
   d. stage

Page 69

1. a. Circle: tasks

   Underline: faire des photocopies / coller des timbres / poster les lettres / ranger le bureau

   b. Circle: sandwich course

   Underline: c'est-à-dire à la fois des cours au lycée professionnel et travailler dans l'entreprise

   c. Circle: bitter

   Underline: souriante / enthousiaste

   d. Circle: to take on

   Underline: m'employer

2. a. Clues: some are already famous / have played in many films / for some it's their first role E

   Translation: vedettes: stars (actors / actresses)

   b. Clue: donné (prizes given) S

   Translation: décerné: given / awarded

   c. Clue: mécontents (unhappy) A

   Translation: ravis: delighted / happy

   d. Clues: Oscar, Lion d'or, Bafta Ex

   Translation: récompenses: awards / prizes

Page 70

1. a. **dés**ordre = disorder = in a mess/untidy

   déplacer = displace = to move

   irréparables = **ir**reparable/beyond repair

   illisibles = unreadable = illegible

   impatiente = impatient

   mécontente = discontented/displeased

   injuste = unjust/unfair

   malheureuse = unhappy

   b. **re**faire = to do again, to make again, more

   reprendre = to take again/have some more

   relu (relire) = reread

   recommencé (recommencer) = start again

   réorganiser = reorganise

   c. **pré**vois (prévoir) = to 'see before' = to intend/envisage

   préhistoire = prehistory

   prédestiné = predestined

2. a. appréhensif (quality) = apprehensive

   chaleureux (quality / character) = warm/welcoming

   b. animalerie (place) = pet shop

   biscuiterie (place) = biscuit factory

   c. gentillesse (characteristic/quality) = gentil = kind/ness

   franchise (characteristic/quality) = franc = frank/ness

   loyauté (characteristic/quality) = loyalty

   curiosité (characteristic/quality) = curiosity

   d. météorologiques (adjective, to do with météo/weather) = meteorological

   volcanique (adjective) = volcanic

   séismique (adjective, to do with earthquake) = seismic

   catastrophiques (adjective) = catastrophic

   e. calculette = little (pocket) calculator

   chemisette = light/summer shirt

   camionnette = little lorry/van

3. a. in**amical** = unfriendly

   b. re**froid**issement = getting cold / cooling

   c. a**grand**ir = make bigger

   d. en**registr**er = to register / record

   e. dé**courage**ant = discouraging

Page 71

Exam-style question

		Problem	Reason
1	at the beginning	boss angry	clumsy / broke a lot of stuff
2	work at the bar	clients couldn't drink the cocktails / cocktails undrinkable	knew nothing about alcohol
3	wages	badly paid	boss was dishonest / kept all the tips

Page 72

Exam-style question

1 parce qu' il avait plaisir / aimait retrouver toute sa famille
2 la propreté de la maison / impressionner ses invités
3 parce que les visiteurs apportaient tous des (pochettes de) bonbons et gâteaux
4 les vêtements de sa grand-mère étaient immettables / trop grands – il devait les porter par politesse pour sa grand-mère

Page 73

Page 66 exam-style question

1	Grandfather	can't collect as much honey	bees killed by pesticides
2	Village	air pollution	factory
3	Older people	cannot travel	less public transport

Page 67 exam-style question

1 un bulletin correct / de bonnes notes / de bonnes appréciations
2 elle n'aime pas les SVT / elle pense que les SVT, c'est inintéressant / ce n'est pas intéressant; elle a aimé les activités extrascolaires
3 longues répétitions deux fois par semaine; c'était dur d'apprendre le texte
4 c'est/c'était normal d'avoir le trac / d'avoir peur

Answers

Notes